LIVING LIFE AGAINST THE ODDS

A PERSONAL CHRONICLE

REGINALD A. BODDIE

Fulton Books
Meadville, PA

Published by Fulton Books 2021

ISBN 978-1-64952-181-1 (paperback)
ISBN 978-1-63710-663-1 (hardcover)
ISBN 978-1-64952-182-8 (digital)

Printed in the United States of America

DEDICATION

This book was written to chronicle my life, with hope that it might inspire others never to give up regardless of the challenges faced in life. This book is dedicated to my mother, Gladys Boddie, who helped instill in me strong principles, unwavering determination, and a positive spirit. My mother passed on August 3, 2008, in Clearwater, Florida, after waging a vigorous battle against pancreatic cancer for eight years, defying medical predictions and perhaps history. She also made history before the US Supreme Court as a plaintiff in *Boddie v. State of Connecticut,* securing access to the courts for indigent persons through fee waivers, and fought fervently for improving conditions in public housing. She cared tremendously about people and the human condition. My mother was truly my hero and friend.

I also dedicate this book to Charisse Boddie, my wife, friend, and soul mate, who saved my life twice when I was in denial about being seriously ill and hesitant to go to the hospital. I also thank my sister, Gwendolyn Boddie-Bethea, and the many friends who have given me invaluable advice and support throughout my life and professional career. I am deeply indebted to all of you. Thank you for your love, friendship, and generosity.

CONTENTS

INTRODUCTION

Reginald Boddie is a justice of the New York State Supreme Court and former supervising judge of the New York City Civil Court, in Brooklyn, New York. He is a graduate of Brown University and Northeastern University School of Law. Born in New Haven, Connecticut, and raised in the public housing projects there, he shares his experiences of growing up in a poor neighborhood, attending public schools, a stay in a state-operated children's home, his challenges with standardized testing, cancer, temporary blindness, and his rise to become a judge. In this autobiography, Reggie shares information directed at encouraging people to find the best within themselves while reminding them to allow their spirituality to be a persistent guide.

Reggie is admitted to practice law before the New York State and District of Columbia Bars, the federal courts of the Eastern and Southern Districts of New York, the Second Circuit Court of Appeals, and the Supreme Court of the United States. Prior to serving as a judge, he practiced law as an attorney for over twenty years and worked as a volunteer instructor of law education in the New York City Public Schools; a volunteer attorney for the New York City Civil Court Volunteer Lawyers' Project; the founder, president, and executive director of United Youth Enterprises Inc., a youth leadership organization; a board member of the Boys and Girls' Clubs; and a project director with the New York City Bar Justice Center, among many other activities.

Reggie is a member of numerous bar associations and previously served as a member of the Democratic Judicial Screening Committee for Kings and Richmond Counties in New York City. He is the recipient of a host of awards and professional recognition, including Who's Who in the World, Who's Who in America, Who's Who in American Law, Who's Who Albert N. Marquis Lifetime Achievement Award, New York City Civil Court Volunteer Lawyer of the Year Award, New York State Courts Pro Bono Service Award, African American Trailblazer Award, Kings County Courts Special Achievement Award, the Catholic Lawyers Guild Hon. William T. Bellard Judiciary Award, Kings County Housing Court Bar Association Judiciary Award of Merit, and NAACP Public Service Award, among others.

He is married to Charisse Boddie.

CHAPTER 1

Growing Up in New Haven

I was born on Flag Day, June 14, 1959, at Grace New Haven Hospital in New Haven, Connecticut. The hospital would eventually be renamed Yale New Haven Hospital in recognition of its affiliation with Yale University. Yale University had grown tremendously since these early days to consume large sections of the New Haven metropolitan area and would play a major role in New Haven politics.

My mother was married to John Boddie, which is where I derived my last name. However, I could rarely recall him being present for any extended period of time in my life. My mother eventually would have six children, three boys and three girls: David, Gwendolyn, Sonia, Carla, Ronald, and me. I am the third oldest.

As a youngster, I attended Woolsey School, in the Fair Haven section of New Haven until the second grade. I remember best my first day in kindergarten when my mother took me to school. When she departed, I cried a lot. The teacher, Ms. Connelly, comforted me. After that, I thoroughly enjoyed going to school daily and playing educational games with my new friends, drinking milk, eating crackers or cookies for snack, and learning my ABCs. I was proud of learning my ABCs faster than most of the children in my class. Not only did I learn the alphabets quickly, I was able to recite them backwards. My first year in school passed quickly.

I also remember the following year in first grade. I developed a strong attraction for reading, making a challenge of advancing quickly through what was then known as the *Weekly Reader*, always trying to stay ahead of my classmates or in the top group. I also remember vividly my first-grade teacher slamming my hand on the desk in an effort to force me to switch writing left-handed to right-handed. When I told my mother of this incident, she was furious and demanded to visit the teacher. I rarely recall seeing my mother so angry. I pleaded with her not to confront the teacher, but she refused to have it any other way. After my mother confronted the teacher, the teacher never tried to switch my preference again and was extremely courteous to me throughout the remainder of the year. However, my writing would never be smooth after, due to my constant experimentation with trying to write with my right hand and making a concerted effort to determine whether I really was predetermined to be a lefty.

As most left-handed youngsters of my generation can readily recall, we were constantly reminded of our left-handed status virtually every day because of the position of the pencil sharpener mounted on the wall and the orientation of the desks with the table portion mounted on the right side. Consequently, although I was reluctant to have my mother confront the teacher about slamming my hand on the desk for fear of retribution, the fact that she did made me feel I had won a victory for left-handed people. Although unaware at the time, my mother would prove an ardent and courageous fighter whenever and wherever she felt an injustice existed. For this quality, among many others, I have always admired her.

My initial years growing up in New Haven during the 1960s would also be memorable, because at that time young children could walk to school alone, as I often did, without worry of being accosted by strangers. Then my family lived on Haven Street, less than a quarter mile from the schools my brothers, sisters and I attended. Haven Street was a quiet street where every family knew one another and helped with whatever they could, whether offering a small cup of sugar, babysitting, or just good conversation. And at that time, my brothers, sisters, and I knew well not to misbehave in the street because the neighbors were always watching and had unfettered permission to smack our behinds. These times were very different from today. Adults were free to discipline other children at will. And if parents learned of the misbehavior, they would repeat the treat by smacking our behinds. This was an inducement for us to behave even outside the presence of our parents. Consequently, when we misbehaved outside the home, we begged the adults not to tell our parents for fear of further retribution.

I was rarely the recipient of such treatment since I did not like being embarrassed in public or in the presence of my brothers and sisters at home. But I still remember the day I spoke out to my mother and ran out the house. She threatened to impress upon me the need to keep my mouth shut when her friend Shirley arrived. Shirley was a close friend of my mother and the least favorite of my brothers, sisters and I because Shirley had mastered the art of embarrassing and beating children in public.

We often referred to her as the queen of abuse and ridicule. She reprimanded her children in my family's presence about the most embarrassing topics, whether it was the need to wash their bodies or to stop wetting the bed. Her comments were raw. I often felt embarrassed for her children. Shirley was simply tactless. Once she told her son to go into the bathroom and wash the rings off his penis. Although very young at the time, even I knew that was impossible. Consequently, I wondered why she would go to such great lengths to embarrass her children in front of me and my siblings.

Shirley also beat her children regularly and bragged about the effectiveness of the beatings. Consequently, her children usually behaved in her presence and acted out in her absence. Thus, I often wondered whether Shirley's behavior led to the children having any greater respect for her. Although this question lingered frequently on my mind, I never inquired of her children because it was a very sensitive topic.

Needless to say, I was terrified when our one family house on Haven Street was condemned by the City of New Haven due to the landlord's neglect to perform repairs, and I learned that we would be moving into the public housing projects where Shirley resided on Ashmun Street. After all, it was Shirley who suggested that my mother start putting a switch to my behind to stop my tantrums when I could not get my way. My tantrums, though rare, sometimes even stunned me. After one of the tantrums, Shirley hit me with a switch so hard on my belly that it left a permanent marking. Unfortunately, I would wear that scar for the rest of my life and be questioned about it by every doctor who examined me without a shirt. But in those days, you dared not report your mother or her friends to the police. Thus, I quickly learned to remain silent about the mark. The pain of being reminded about that day was simply too much to lay bare. Yet I never forgot.

I do not condone child abuse, but at that time the lines between discipline and abuse were so blurred that a child would, in most circumstances, be ignored. Such was the case when my sister Sonia ran away the year before. My mother had the police locate Sonia and spanked her in front of the police as my siblings and I watched. Thus, I had no reason to believe the result would have been any different in my case.

My brothers and sisters did not want to move close to Shirley either, although we had no choice, except for my brother David. David is my oldest brother. While still a teenager, my mother arranged for David to attend the Albany Boys' School in Albany, New York, in an effort to keep him off the streets. David had been a frequent visitor to the local juvenile detention center. Eventually my mother grew tired of going to the center and arranged for David to be sent out of state to attend school and join a better group of friends.

Although this appeared to be a difficult choice for my mother, as judged by her sullen manner for the entire year after David left, she tried to put up a strong front. She also chided the rest of us that if we decided to follow David's example and landed in detention, she would not visit us. Her persistence paid off. Later, when one or more of my siblings landed in the juvenile detention center in downtown New Haven for a day, she left them to contemplate the circumstances the entire weekend. They never returned. David himself graduated from the Albany Boys' School and continued to Syracuse University, where he received a bachelor's degree. He later attended Texas Southern University Law School and became the first lawyer and judge in the family. Thus, David avoided all the chaos that would later come with our family's move closer to Shirley.

I was preparing to start third grade when the family moved to Ashmun Street. Suddenly my life of comfort in a single-family home with a spacious backyard and grape vines disappeared. Gone also were my regular visits with Reverend Robert E. Jones of the Fair Haven Parents' Ministry, then a divinity student at Yale University, who often took me out on weekends and kept my attention on positive activities. Also gone were my weekday visits to Farnam Neighborhood House after school, where I met Robert Sheeley and Mark Malley, who together served as mentors during these early years and with whom I remain in touch.

I had enjoyed living on Haven Street, a neighborhood of single and multiple family homes with residents from diverse racial backgrounds. At that time, Haven Street was a very quiet neighborhood with close neighbors, where everyone, adults and children, looked after each other. My family rented the entire house at 72 Haven Street. I enjoyed the spacious rooms in the three-level single-family home. The house had a full basement, a fully accessible attic, two main floors, and a large backyard. There was ample space to play in the house and backyard. And when I grew tired of being in the house, I could walk nearby to visit friends who had similar space to play.

My mother warned that one day we might have to move due to the landlord's failure to make repairs. My understanding then was simply that my mother paid monthly for use of the house and the absentee landlord refused to make repairs. I did not fully comprehend the repairs my mother was referencing. I also did not recall ever meeting the landlord. However, eventually our house was condemned by the city, and my life of relative comfort was replaced by a small apartment on the eighth floor of a crowded poorly maintained federally subsidized high-rise building in a neighborhood of similar developments. In place of my spacious living abode, I found myself relegated to a small three-bedroom apartment in a high-rise building, where I would share a small room with my younger brother, Ronald.

On Ashmun Street, or in the Elm Haven projects as they were better known, there were few two-parent households, high crime, and the building hallways and adjoining streets were filthy. As I gradually learned, these conditions existed in great measure not for lack of many residents trying or having ambitious dreams and goals but because the neighborhood was not allocated the same resources of other neighborhoods I visited, particularly those where many of my White friends resided. Nevertheless, the families were determined to succeed with the limited resources available, both financially and otherwise. Still, it was extremely rare for people who grew up in my predominantly Black neighborhood to go to college, and worse, they were not expected to.

When I arrived on Ashmun Street, I was immediately enrolled at Winchester Community School. Winchester was a public school and the assigned school for my neighborhood and the thousands of youth who resided in the nearby federally subsidized public housing projects, owned and managed by the Housing Authority of the City of New Haven. The student population at Winchester was predominantly Black, reflecting the composition of the neighborhood.

During my first weeks in the neighborhood, I was forced by an older teenager to fight another youth to establish my pecking order. Ironically, being able to fight was considered a precious resource and determined the status of youths in the neighborhood. The fight created a dilemma for me, both because I did not enjoy fighting and because the person I was forced to fight was the cousin of my first new friend, Jesse Phillips. I wondered what would happen if I won. Still, I had to fight because my mother taught all her children that we were to fight if picked on, and if we did not win and came home crying, she would repeat the act. So, I hustled and tussled, although my heart beat heavily in fear of what Jesse might do to me if I won.

Determined not to lose, I beat Jesse's cousin, and surprisingly my friendship with Jesse Phillips was sealed. We became the best of friends. Later, Morris Trent Jr., Kenneth Jenkins, and Robert Harriott Jr. joined the group by the same process. We established a solid group of good fighters, even though none of us really enjoyed fighting.

One can only imagine the shock on my face when I returned to Connecticut more recently for a funeral of Jesse's sister and witnessed the same bully that forced me to fight Jesse's cousin playing bass in a band at the church funeral. I could not believe my eyes. This experience once again reconfirmed for me the power of prayer. I always thought my bully could do some good one day. I just never envisioned him being at the altar of any church. But there he was, in front of the church playing the bass guitar and singing praises to God. It was a profound vision and soothing to my heart and soul.

After the service, he approached to compliment me on my achievements. I was surprised and humbled to learn that he followed my transition from the neighborhood. Jesse and I remarked about his past and told him how gratifying it was to see his transition. The gentleman remarked, "I could not have been that bad." We both said in unison, "Yes, you were." I was just so delighted to see another example of how prayer works and God's intervention on his behalf. And I must say, he is an outstanding musician and leader of the band. I felt extremely blessed to witness his new talents being used in a house of worship, all to the glory of God.

My friend Morris Trent Jr., who attended the event, also went on to become a well-established professional musician in Connecticut. Kenneth Jenkins works at a retirement and rehabilitation facility. Robert Harriott Jr. became a minister and works with an ambulette company, and Jesse Phillips established a career in the military.

During the early days, we spent countless hours together playing basketball and football, attending parties, school, and trying our hand at singing. I was not much of a basketball player, but I was effective enough to score important points and to mount a reasonable challenge. However, most of the children who frequented the basketball courts learned to master the game and were often chosen for teams ahead of me. Still, I was proud of my basketball skills and even played on the local YMCA team, though we were never champions.

I fared better with football. I could run, hit, and tackle opponents. I was effective at the game and a force to be reckoned with. I enjoyed the game a great deal, although I did not like the injuries that sometimes came with it. Such was the case when I played tackle football in my building hallway at 225 Ashmun Street. It was winter, and many children hung out in the hallways to avoid the cold weather playing tops, marbles, tag, or hallway football. On this day, my friends and I were playing a leisure game of touch football when I bumped heads with Jesse, sending me to the hospital for stitches above my eye. Fortunately, my eyebrows masked the scar until adulthood when the scar sought to peek through again. On another occasion, I snagged my leg on an outdoor fence going for the touchdown pass. I eventually stopped playing football while in high school after I twisted my leg in a Little League game and learned it was difficult to walk with crutches.

Robert, on the other hand, became a football stand out among our group in Little League football. He joined the League late after some encouragement by me, but he immediately took charge. He could run fast and tackle hard. Little could stop him, including me, even with much more weight on my body. Therefore, after I decided to no longer play football due to my injury, I resorted to attending the games Robert played. They were fascinating to watch, as Robert plowed down others in his way, with little effort.

I also spent many hours with Jesse, Robert, and the members of the group, going to parties. In those days, parties and other recreational activities were our main release from the pressures of school, work, and daily routines. As a result, nearly every weekend we found a party to attend. These events were either held at friends' houses, a school, or one of the local recreation centers. I enjoyed the parties at school and the recreation centers most because they provided ample opportunity for me to meet other people. Even then, I enjoyed meeting people immensely. We had interesting conversations, and I learned new things. I also liked impressing the women with my dance skills.

Initially, Jesse was the true dance master in our group. He learned quickly and could execute almost any dance with precision. I frequently observed him closely and picked up the skill. Before long, I was creating my own version of dances. Eventually I was able to compete with the best of dancers. This provided for better conversation because my friends, male and female, admired men who could dance. At this stage of my life, it also helped enhance my circle of friends and community residents' view of me as someone who had skills, other than just the ability to do well in school. Frankly, the ability to do well in school was not as esteemed in my neighborhood as it should have been, leading to frequent references to me and others like me as bookworms or worse. Consequently, my ability to adapt and show marked success in other areas helped sully the criticism and boost my popularity.

By attending dances and other social events all over the city, I met many new friends and eventually grew to know the names of hundreds of children in my neighborhood and beyond. In those days, my mother showed great trust and permitted me to roam the different neighborhoods with limited supervision. Consequently, on any given day, I could be seen in any one of several New Haven neighborhoods or towns nearby. We had an understanding that I could exercise such liberties as long as I stayed out of trouble. I understood the enormity of this responsibility and returned the favor by staying out of trouble. My sisters, to their disdain, were more closely monitored.

CHAPTER 2

Journey from Children's Home to Preparatory School

I always did well in school and was never in any trouble of consequence. Still, I resented the depressed condition of the Ashmun Street neighborhood in which my family resided. I especially despised the lack of constructive recreational activity, except for the local community center where fights frequently occurred. I also loathed the urine-infested building hallways, the large amounts of trash on the streets, and the overcrowding. I yearned for better. Approximately three years after my family moved to Ashmun Street, my mother informed me and my siblings that she decided to send Sonia to a children's home because she was out of control. I begged to follow thinking the experience would be a good vacation from the neighborhood.

I was about to enter the sixth grade, and my family was on public assistance, although my mother would soon complete high school at night in the adult education program at Wilbur Cross High School and began a long career as a nurse's aide at St. Raphael Hospital. The State Receiving Home, as it was known, was state operated and funded and located at Warehouse Point, in Windsor, Connecticut, near the state capitol. Going to the home voluntarily proved to be one of the most educational decisions in my life.

Although as a child I always received good grades and my behavior was usually good, I quickly learned that I had volunteered to live in a home for bad children. Most of the children had been placed in the home because they had gotten into trouble with the police or were abandoned by their parents. Though my situation was entirely different, after my arrival, the State refused to permit me to return home, except once monthly on weekends. Unknown to me at the time and perhaps my mother as well, judging from her subsequent battle for my return later, she had signed me over as a ward of the State. Years later, my mother told me that she was reluctant to let me go but relented since I insisted and bared the emotional pain. I was shocked to hear this since my mother was such a strong person and few things troubled her.

The home was a real eye-opening experience since I was required to call people who had no blood relationship to me Mom and Pop, wear institutionalized clothes, and attend a school with teachers who clearly did not think Black people had any intellect, as evidenced by some of the questions they asked: "Do Black people believe in God?" and "Do you read?"

I was raised in the church. My mother also had insisted that all her children began reading at a young age. I especially liked to read the encyclopedia. I enjoyed the large amounts of information contained in them. Therefore, I found the inquiry to be very demeaning and to evidence a lack of any meaningful exposure to Black people. I also found it demeaning to be required to call the resident caretakers at the home Mom and Pop. These people clearly were not my mother or father and consisted, in most instances, of an entirely different ancestry. It was especially annoying to be required to call someone Pop when I had never met my biological father.

Also annoying was the fact that all the children in my dormitory had to go everywhere together. We went to school, outside to play, to the cafeteria, and even to the showers together. All my freedom was gone, including choosing what I wanted to eat. One day, I decided I did not want to eat hot oatmeal. I do not recall the reason, except that I never really liked eating hot cereals unless I was truly starving, which remains true to this day. That day, a couple, Mr. and Mrs. Pat Riley, oversaw the dormitory. Mr. Riley did not take lightly to my refusal to eat the oatmeal, although normally it was of no concern if the children ate. When we returned to the dormitory shortly after, he punched me and repeatedly stomped on my leg with his feet for my refusal to obey his request to eat the oatmeal. He kicked and stomped on my leg as if I was a rag doll. His foot hurt tremendously. And no one came to my aid, even as I screamed out in pain. I recognized this as child abuse, just as I had when Shirley beat me, but there was little I could do. However, unlike Shirley, Mr. Riley had been hired by the State to protect me, and he abused me with impunity.

Instead of lashing out, I resorted to praying as my mother taught all her children. She required us to attend church every Sunday. We thought it was to save our souls so we would behave. Therefore, initially we did not like attending church. However, she did not permit us to go outside to play on Sundays unless we attended church. And when she was not present to watch us, she got a report from her friends at church. Therefore, praying was not new to me. And although I did not like being forced to attend church, I learned a great deal in the process, often mimicking the preacher when I arrived home and thinking that maybe one day I, too, would become a preacher.

The night after the beating incident, I prayed and begged God for an answer, and he provided it. I needed to develop a plan. I developed a plan which was to first tell my social worker about the abuse and, if Mr. Riley was not fired, tell my mother. I told the social worker, and he refused to take any action. Feeling helpless and betrayed, I told my mother. She threatened to come to the school to "kill that evil man." She came to the school and spoke to my social worker and the director about the abuse and their failure to act. Also angered, she begged me to show her the man who stomped on me. Fortunately for him, he was not at work that day. I feared what my mother might have done. Still, Mr. Riley obviously got the message because he was kind to me after. But I found myself unable to forgive someone who would abuse a child in that manner.

I remained at the State Receiving Home for one year, but it felt like eternity. During that period, time seemed to stand still. Every day consisted of the same routine, except the rare weekend when we went away to play sports, roller-skate, or bowl. I made clear to my mother and the State that I had agreed to go voluntarily, and I wanted to return home. I gained a lot of value out of being in the State Receiving Home, but I yearned to return to New Haven. While there, I witnessed firsthand what it might feel like for people who got into trouble and were sentenced to imprisonment. This is because the home felt like a children's prison, and we frequently visited Connecticut's major adult male prisons, Somers and Enfield, to play baseball and basketball to entertain the inmates.

Whenever we visited Somers and Enfield, we were required to relinquish all our belongings, subject to search, and pass through electric gates that we were given stern warnings not to touch. We passed corridors containing multiple jail cells. The heavy corridor doors were locked behind us as we passed through each unit. Eventually, we arrived at the field surrounded by hundreds of inmates, as we played our games under the huge shining lights. At the conclusion of the games, we were treated to dessert in the cafeteria and repeated the process in reverse.

Even then, I saw no value in having young children visit a prison to entertain the inmates.

Consequently, I often wondered what message the State was trying to convey to us. I hoped the message was that we did not want to grow up to be in a real prison. If that was the message, it was well received on my behalf, although I never engaged in a discussion with the other children about my thoughts. At the time, I was just happy to have had some time away from the home.

But for all intents and purposes, as far as I was concerned, I had been to a prison-like environment without ever having committed a crime. The only things that kept me sane throughout this experience were the frequent letters of encouragement from Robert and Jean Sheeley, my friends from Farnam Neighborhood House, monthly visits home, prayer, and development of a conscious effort to get out.

Little did I know at the time, Robert Sheeley, whom I warmly refer to as Bob, probably did not approve of me going to the State Receiving Home. Yet he never shared his views with me until years later. Instead, he offered to adopt me on one of my visits to his home. I was truly honored by the offer and exuberant expression of love. I have always loved him and his wife, Jean, dearly, but I did not accept the offer because I felt it would be a betrayal to my mother. I also wondered what his family and I would experience having to deal with the fact that he was Irish and I, African American. I also understood that children cost money, and he and his wife already had two children of their own to care for. So, I respectfully told him as much as I love his family, I was not ready to do that. Nevertheless, he has always served as a surrogate father to me, and I am grateful for it.

Still, I was determined to go home. After I made clear my intentions of returning home to my mother and the state social worker, the State came up with a plan to get me out of the State Receiving Home by sending me to another school, Becket Academy. Becket Academy, located in East Haddam, Connecticut, at that time was a prestigious private preparatory school for wealthy White youths. But if this was my only way to return home, I was willing to give it a chance. After all, the Connecticut State Welfare Department had chosen a small number of youths, like me, to experiment in a summer program at Becket to see if we could compete with wealthy White children. I have always liked a challenge, so I accepted the offer as a condition to going home at the end of the summer if I did not desire to stay. The State reluctantly agreed.

I interviewed with the headmaster of Becket and was told what to expect from the school and what was expected from me. The bottom line was I would be among a very small number of Black children from poor neighborhoods. We would have a strict schedule beginning eight o'clock in the morning with breakfast, church services, followed by class, lunch, more classes, dinner, brief free time, and a study hall from 7:00 to 8:00 p.m. in the evening. This pattern would be repeated most days, except Sunday. I would be among the best and brightest academically. The State would pay my huge bill, and if I did well, I might be offered the opportunity to remain during the upcoming academic year. And with this agreement, I left the State Receiving Home, leaving Sonia behind to join what was then an all-male student body at Becket Academy in East Haddam, Connecticut.

At Becket, religion was strongly emphasized, as well as academic achievement.

Every morning began with prayer in the school chapel. I felt very comfortable in church. I left the church each day feeling renewed and that God was watching over me, although the prayer format was vastly different from my Baptist upbringing. I made many friends at Becket and found that although there were few Black people, the White students, most of whom never had any exposure to Black people, respected us for who we were. Unfortunately, this was not always true about the adults at Becket.

When I first arrived at Becket, I was given an IQ test to determine my placement in class and told that I scored poorly. While my initial thought was to guess whether something really was wrong with me, I challenged the person who told me to explain why I scored low while always doing well academically. No explanation was forthcoming. Thus, I concluded even then that something was amiss with the test, and I just simply did not test well on certain standardized tests. But I could not permit Becket to mark me for failure, especially at such a young age. This news greatly contradicted how I viewed myself—smart, gifted, and prepared to make great contributions to the world.

Since Becket could offer no explanation for the contradiction, I challenged the school to place me in a rigorous class and assess my performance. I agreed if I did not perform satisfactorily to be placed in a less challenging class. Becket took me up on the challenge and placed me in a top class where students were given daily time tests. I performed near the top of the class each time. The more challenges they gave me, the more I delivered, and eventually the school let me remain in the top class. Both my teachers and I were impressed. I achieved wonderfully at Becket and made many friends. My teachers, in turn, gloated over my success and my prospects for the future. I truly enjoyed the experience.

It was while at Becket that I learned for the first time about the many luxuries wealthy people have: never having to worry about money, travel, vacations, fine dining, etc.

My friends at Becket often shared with me stories about their families' wealth, the different professionals that frequented their homes, the expensive cars their parents drove, and the lofty places they visited while on vacation. Then, it was hard to fathom such wealth amid the impoverished environment in which I had lived. I could not help but wonder how our experiences and circumstances resulted in such stark differences.

Even then, I knew many diligent working families and some very successful people, but no one I knew had reached that level of wealth. And if they had, I certainly was not aware of it. While many people contemplating these circumstances might have asked themselves, "What's wrong with me?" I never did. However, I must make a point here of noting my friends at Becket and their parents were very generous in inviting me to go on vacation with them whenever a weekend break arose. I spent several days with them locally and enjoyed it, but I was more excited about visiting my friends in New Haven.

At the conclusion of the summer session, Becket offered me a full scholarship to continue at the school in September. I was truly honored by the offer, as well as the experience I acquired, but I yearned to return home to New Haven, where I could converse with a more racially and economically diverse group of people. I simply was not comfortable hanging out almost entirely with very wealthy people.

CHAPTER 3

Transitioning Back to the Neighborhood after Preparatory School

When I next visited New Haven, I shared my plan of returning home with my mother. Initially, she was uncomfortable with me returning home because she thought it could only lead to trouble since I would be assigned to the neighborhood public school, Troup Middle School, for seventh grade, where fights occurred nearly every day. However, I was able to get her to agree to permit me to attend a Catholic school. This plan, however, failed when we learned that St. Martin De Porres School, where my brother Ronald and sister Carla were enrolled, did not have any spaces available. So once again, I was stuck. But I refused to give up. I felt that my life and future depended on coming up with another plan and to do so immediately.

After the Catholic school option failed, I begged my mother to permit me to return home and attend Troup School for seventh grade if I agreed to consistently maintain honors. I thought it would be easy to maintain high grades since I always had good grades. But it made the point that I was not going to let the environment at the school destroy my future, because I was different. My mother accepted the proposal and added the condition that I enroll at the school on my own. However, in those days it was unusual for a child to enroll himself in school. Parents escorted their children to school the first day. I plead with my mother to enroll me, but she refused.

25

My first day at Troup, the new students were assembled in a classroom. The principal John Esposito called the children's names and announced the class assignments. At one point, he interrupted the roll call and asked my name. When I told him, he remarked, "I don't see your name on the roster. Where are your parents?" I responded, "May I discuss this with you in your office after you finish?" He agreed. Minutes later, we met in his office. I fully explained my circumstances, the fact that my mother did not want me to attend the school, the reasons, and the compact I made with her to enroll myself. He responded by calling my mother to verify what I told him and completed the paperwork for me.

He also told me if ever I needed assistance with anything not to hesitate to come see him. He meant it. From that day forward, Mr. Esposito and I became very good friends. Upon graduating from Troup, I followed his career, and we stayed in touch, even as he progressed to become a candidate for mayor of the city of New Haven. I continued visiting him until I graduated college. He was always sincere and encouraging, a friend I will never forget.

I also met Dr. Reginald Mayo at Troup. Reginald Mayo agreed to assist me academically if ever I had trouble with my studies. He insisted that I succeed since we shared the same name. I admired Reginald Mayo because he was the chairman of the science department. This was a rare title for any Black person in New Haven's public schools at that time because New Haven did not have significant numbers of Black teachers. Dr. Mayo eventually rose from the ranks of teacher to become the first Black superintendent of the New Haven Public Schools, after the reign of another close friend of mine, his predecessor, Dr. Gerald Tirozzi. I was not surprised.

I met many wonderful students at Troop and learned a great deal academically. Although Troop had a predominantly Black student body, consisting mostly of youngsters from low-income families, it also had high-achiever classes similar to Becket Academy. I was in several of the classes and was challenged by fellow students, both male and female, who were equally bright or better. I also found the teachers at Troup, with rare exception, to be extremely committed. This made my transition home easier, except I had to either stay at school late to avoid the bad kids who wanted to fight or leave with the other students and look over my shoulder all the way home. I usually waited until most students left. I also enrolled in the school band, which rehearsed late in the school day or after school to keep busy. Initially, I tried my hand at playing the trumpet and found it difficult to blow notes. I then tried the baritone, which was comfortable, and eventually moved on to the trombone. I found that I really enjoying playing instruments and especially the hit songs I heard on the radio. I quickly found myself hanging out with others who similarly enjoyed the experience.

After school, I usually studied at home while most of my friends were outside playing. This was not an easy feat since I could see the children on the playground from my apartment window on the eight floor. However, I refused to let this distract me. My priorities were established, and I was confident and motivated in my quest to succeed because I was determined to go to college and acquire a better station in life, as had my older brother David. I desired a professional career, a family, and a comfortable home.

Despite good intentions, I had two memorable scuffles at Troup. The first involved a young man who tried stealing my sneakers out of my hand to prove I would not fight. With my maleness at stake, or so I thought, I showed him he could not mess with me. As a result, I was required to do after school detention for one week. It seemed like eternity. The second event was even more memorable because I learned some strong lessons from it. I was involved in a fight in the science class of a teacher I admired after a student picked on me. By taking the bait, I had disappointed the teacher since I was a favorite and showed my own weakness in the process.

The student I fought was sent home for detention. However, my mother refused to permit the assistant principal William Beatty to send me home because she felt this would reward me with a vacation while punishing her by being required to locate a babysitter or take time off from work to supervise me. Mr. Beatty relented and required me to clean his office, scrub the walls and all else. They proved their point. It was humiliating. All the other students observing this teased me incessantly. I made sure I never got into trouble at school again.

My mother used the same technique on my brothers and sisters, effectively denying them any time off from school for their disruptive behavior. You would have thought she had taken more than a few courses in psychology. Still, I excelled at Troup and graduated with honors, as promised. By the time I graduated from Troup, my mother had already moved off public assistance and acquired full-time employment as a nurse's aide at St. Raphael's Hospital in New Haven, where she continued until retirement.

I truly cherished the fact that my mother worked, but I rarely got to spend much time with her because she often worked the 3:00 p.m.–11:00 p.m. shift and was gone by the time I arrived home. Therefore, my sister Gwendolyn took on most of the responsibility of ensuring that things went smoothly at home while my mother was away. This caused more than a little sibling rivalry since my siblings and I tried, at every turn, to make clear to Gwendolyn that she was not our mother. Still, she demanded and received tremendous respect, even if she had to force it out of us. Consequently, during my younger years in junior high school, while my mother was away at work, after studying, I often stayed at my friends' houses in the neighborhood until bedtime before going home.

While my mother was usually occupied with work weekdays, my brothers, sisters, and I always looked forward to the weekly weekend dinners with her at the various restaurants in town, where we delighted in eating spaghetti and meatballs, chicken or fried fish, or a seafood combination while updating her on our progress at school or the neighborhood gossip. I also looked forward to our monthly outings to the drive-in theater, where we delighted in seeing our favorite movie picks, or hers, while chomping on the homemade hero sandwiches and popcorn she brought along. And she always seemed to have a drink ready for us, which was readily retrieved from her storage of drinks secretly tucked away in the rear compartment of her station wagon.

My mother really knew how to save a dollar. She was not willing to spend any money at the movie concession stands. Whatever we needed to comfort us at the movies, she was prepared to provide. We once thought we could out smart her and wind our way to the concession stand like all the other children and asked for ice cream. We knew she could not possibly have stored such in her car or brought it along in her fancy packages. She responded, "It's waiting for you in the refrigerator at home." We gave up after that. In restaurants, before refills became popular, my mother did not believe in wasting money on ice when the soda was already cold. She politely requested that all our drinks be made without ice. And you did not want to give her the end of a tomato, it would immediately be sent back to the kitchen.

My mother also had elegant taste. Whenever she went out, she was elegantly dressed. She dressed all of us similarly. She also went to school to become a tailor and made most of my sisters' clothes. She attended auto mechanic school to learn to fix her car, long before woman mechanics became popular. When I inquired of her interest in this regard, she indicated she had grown tired of male mechanics overcharging her for car repairs. I had heard so many of these complaints from women I could not question that premise. Moreover, unlike many men, I eventually learned most of my auto mechanic skills from my mother. She was a woman far ahead of her time.

My brothers and sisters would emulate many of my mother's skills. Gwendolyn and Carla eventually followed my mother into nursing, working as a registered nurse and licensed practical nurse respectively. Gwendolyn also sewed all her children's clothes. Ronald, although becoming a postman, also learned to sew and gained notoriety outfitting weddings in the New Haven area. Sonia always insisting on being a standout among the crowd, after working a short-term for a Yale University dining hall departed to assert her social activist skills, advocating the issues of the day with various organizations at the State Capitol in Hartford. David and I too would eventually pick up the advocates for justice "bug" of our mother.

During summers, I spent all my time at different camps to stay occupied. I enjoyed Camp Farnam, which was operated by Farnam Neighborhood House on Fillmore Street, most. I began attending Camp Farnam at age five, when I lived in Fair Haven, and continued when I moved to Ashmun Street. Camp Farnam was located in Durham, Connecticut, about a half hour outside New Haven in an area consisting predominantly of farmland. On the route to camp, I thoroughly enjoyed the bus ride singing songs along the way or just chatting with my friends, the fresh air, farms and farm animals clearly in view.

Children from different cities and towns attended Camp Farnam. We had a wonderful time swimming, boating, participating in arts and crafts, and other activities. I met many friends of all races and economic status at the camp, and I thoroughly enjoyed it. I did all that I could to return every year. After I aged out as a regular camper, I commenced working at the camp as a teenager in conjunction with the summer youth employment program and continued until college, holding positions as a pool maintenance person, lifeguard, swimming instructor, and pool director.

As pool director and swimming instructor, I cherished supervising the lifeguards at the camp both in the pool area and the nearby lake, where boating classes were held. I also enjoyed tremendously teaching the campers swimming skills from basics of swimming to advanced skills. While teaching the campers swimming or boating skills, I loved engaging them in discussions on their view of the world. On occasion, they would share more personal matters that caused anxiety at home, and I would encourage them in constructive ways of addressing the issues. I found the more receptive I was to their concerns, the more open they were to trust me both in and out of the water.

I recall two situations I encountered that best illustrate this point. The first involved two young children whose parents were divorcing. The children felt they contributed to their parents arguing all the time and asked what they could do to improve the situation. I informed them that just as young people do not always get along, it is the same for parents, and they should not feel it is their fault. After, they conceded other personal matters with me. They grew much more comfortable in my classes and at camp in general. Weeks later their parents visited the camp for parent day. Meeting me for the first time, they were shocked and stated three times, "You are Reggie?" to which I responded yes. I asked why. They responded that their children talked about me all the time. I feigned as if I did not know why, but I knew the children had been comforted by me, and the parents were surprised to see that they had grown so comfortable with a very young guy. But I knew the children only saw me as Reggie, the kind guy who they could talk to as a friend, and I was happy to oblige.

The same day, I also met a single mother of three of my students, two girls and a boy.

I had become friendly with all the siblings, but only the older daughter was in my advanced class. Though extremely smart and always performing at the top of the class, she often admitted not reading my swimming books as suggested prior to written examinations for the class. I could not wait to meet her mother to find out whether this habit carried over to the child's work in school. Like the first parents, this mother, too, was shocked to see who I was, but she was more personable.

She, too, explained that her children talked about me all the time and invited me to have lunch with the family together at camp. I accepted, and we engaged in wonderful conversation during my lunch break. After, she invited me to visit the children at home anytime. I followed through and became a close friend of the family. Although my relationship continues with the family, unfortunately the mother suffered an untimely death due to a car accident while I was in college.

Camp Farnam fostered a wonderful environment and opportunity for young campers and staff to bond by engaging in exciting activities and new challenges through sports, swimming, crafts, and conversation. My sisters Gwendolyn, Sonia, Carla, and brother Ronald all attended the camp. We cherish the fond memories of our experiences at Camp Farnam, including the overnight stays, where we swam in the pool late at night, roasted marshmallows, sang songs at the campfire, and experienced late night storytelling firsthand. It was truly an unforgettable and rewarding experience.

During summers, my siblings and I also visited relatives in Newport News and Hampton, Virginia, where my mother originated. I enjoyed riding the Greyhound bus, viewing the scenery, and intermingling with people from different cities and states around the country. I also enjoyed listening to the different accents of people and observing their behavior. Most noticeable to me, even as a youngster, was the fast pace of people in the North, as compared to the slow pace in the South. The slower pace allowed me to enjoy nature more and rush less.

Whenever my family and I visited Virginia, our first stop usually was my grandmother's house on Maple Avenue in Hampton, where my sister Gwendolyn and I would climb the tree in the front yard. We loved that big tree, and it presented an opportunity we did not have at home in Connecticut. Our annual ritual after arriving at our grandmother's house was to see who could climb the highest in the tree, which often led to a rebuke by our grandfather if we were caught. But we knew to just stay up in the tree until he departed or come down and stay away from him until his emotion passed. Our grandmother also had a big backyard, but we did not play in the yard since it was occupied by chickens and a garden.

Our grandmother usually had food waiting for us when we finished playing outside. My grandmother's cooking was truly outstanding, and I looked forward to it whenever we visited. Although my grandmother spoke fast and in a heavy Southern accent, I enjoyed talking with her about the progress of my cousins and hearing her expressions of interest in my progress. After this initial welcome, my mother would decide where each of us would stay while in Virginia.

We rarely stayed at my grandmother's house where my mother grew up because the house was very small, although my mother was from a large family. Even during the late 1960s and 1970s, the house contained an outdoor bathroom, which none of us looked forward to using. Consequently, Gwendolyn and I usually stayed at our aunt Jeannette's house, whom we affectionately call Q, while the rest of the family went elsewhere.

With rare exception, we enjoyed our aunts and uncles. However, we persuaded our mother to let us stay with Q because she was younger than most of our other aunts and very funny. She had a wonderful sense of humor, as did her children. She also allowed us a great deal of personal space. We related well to her sons Dwayne and

Earl, who frequently served a role not only as our cousins but also as our personal comedians. We joked about everything throughout our entire stay. They also helped us meet many new friends. Although we visited other cousins in Virginia, Gwendolyn and I grew closest to Earl and Dwayne.

I also relished the fact that my aunt Q, despite raising two children, graduated from Hampton University, one of the nation's premiere historically Black colleges, which at that time was known as Hampton Institute. As a youngster, she was the only person in my family I had known to attend college, until my brother David went to Syracuse University years later. Thus, my aunt Q planted the college seed in my mind early by sharing her yearbook and experiences in college, where she studied and graduated from the nursing school. Although then I did not completely understand the significance of college, hearing her stories made clear it presented an opportunity to meet people from all over the world, gain knowledge and better job opportunities, and my interest was piqued.

I always looked forward to visiting Virginia, although in many respects it appeared behind in time. The Black people we encountered, including many of our own relatives, were still saying "yes, sir" and "yes, ma'am." We, even as children, knew such formalities were no longer mandated. We wondered aloud if they had gotten stuck in a time warp. The neighborhoods in Virginia also remained highly segregated, and there was little interaction among Blacks and Whites, even at public facilities. In the South, during those days, time appeared to have stood still, while the rest of the country moved forward.

My most vivid memory of this fact remains the day my family and I were returning from Newport News on a Greyhound bus in the late 1960s. When we arrived in Richmond, Virginia, we were seated in the back of the bus. My mother had paid for each of our seats. The White driver insisted my mother hold me in her lap and give my seat to a White person. She refused, and he threatened her with arrest. She grew angry and explained that she had a right to the seat, having paid for it, and told him, "Take your ass up there and drive the bus and leave me alone." This was the first time I had heard my mother curse. The people on the bus applauded, but I grew extremely anxious fearing my mother would be arrested. Still, I felt proud of my mother and was glad to have the seat and a window, nonetheless.

The driver did not give up. He threatened to call the police and have them remove us from the bus when we arrived at the depot in Baltimore. When we arrived in Baltimore, the police were waiting. My family and I had visited Baltimore many times before, especially since my stepfather hailed from Baltimore. I had often seen the Baltimore police beat people with sticks, so when the bus arrived at the terminal and I saw the police waiting, I hoped the police would exercise restraint. Although I could see the driver talking to the police through the window, the police never entered the bus, and my mother did not get off the bus as we normally did for snacks. Neither the driver nor the police spoke to my mother. About a half hour later, the bus departed, and we were on our way to New York City.

When the bus departed Baltimore, I immediately felt a great sense of relief because this bus driver's behavior surely would not be tolerated once we headed further north. As a result of this experience, my mother unknowingly had taught me another lesson: be strong, confident, and relentless when confronting injustice. This experience reminded me of how comfortable I had become with the new way of life in the North, although I knew full well that prejudice existed in the North too. The last trip I took to the South by bus was with Gwendolyn alone. We spent a lot of time sharing, observing, and comparing the differences of the North versus the South. It was a fun trip. It helped cement our closeness. Today, we are inseparable.

CHAPTER 4

The High School Challenge

When I graduated Troup Middle School in 1973 and entered Wilbur Cross High School, I was confident and determined to succeed and continue to college. Gwendolyn enrolled at Cross two years before me, and my mother had graduated from the adult night school at Cross and often boasted about all the awards she received. As a result, I was determined to show both Gwendolyn and my mother how well I could perform at Cross. At the time, unless students from the neighborhood chose to attend private school, they were designated to attend the area public schools. My area high school was Cross. The other area high schools were Hillhouse and Lee High School.

I was eager to attend Cross because Cross was the most popular high school at the time and named after a former governor of Connecticut. The school also had a nationally ranked basketball team with Bruce "Soup" Campbell and Jiggy Williamson, the brother of NBA great John Williamson, leading the way, which gave the school additional prestige. Cross also was said, by many, to be the best of the three city public high schools academically. However, this probably depended on who you spoke to because I would eventually meet Constance Baker Motley, the first Black female federal court judge to serve on the US District Court, and learned she graduated from Hillhouse High School. Still, I believed that Cross would provide me the best opportunity for growth, and I was not disappointed.

My first year at Cross was very challenging. I focused intensely on my studies. I also joined the school band, playing the trombone, and worked after school at the Farnam Neighborhood House as a recreational aide. I took courses in algebra, history, expository writing, science, gymnastics, and music. Because the work was more difficult than Troup the year before, I planned my schedule carefully and studied hard.

I especially studied hard for algebra because I did not grasp the concepts quickly. The class was taught by a young Black teacher, Ms. Saundra Stephenson, who was very personable and patient. Consequently, the students in her class felt very comfortable asking her to repeat certain aspects of the lessons, and she was happy to comply. She would eventually help me shed my fear of math, and we became friends for life.

I also had Ms. Billings for writing. Ms. Billings was White and possessed a personality that permitted her to get along with everyone regardless of race or any other traits. She was extremely self-confident and did her best to invoke the same confidence in her students. We shared jokes and talked frankly about mostly any topic. Ms. Billings encouraged excellence, challenging us to write a weekly journal about a selected topic. This exercise challenged us to explore our daily issues and struggles and contemplate our vision for the future. Everyone loved Ms. Billings. I made a habit of trying to visit her classroom everyday even after I completed the course. She was just a wonderful person to know and see in action. She truly enjoyed teaching, and everyone knew it.

Freshman year, I also had Mr. Elwood as a band teacher. Mr. Elwood made clear that all his students were expected to put forth their best, whether we grew up in impoverished neighborhoods or not. He set high goals and expected us to meet them. However, Mr. Elwood would have tantrums. Thus, the challenge of his positions by unruly students might be met with an upturned chair or musical stand, but he made his point. I never dared test Mr. Elwood. I knew he meant well and was unusually committed.

Mr. Elwood took time out of his schedule—day, nights, and weekends—to assist us, and I admired him for that. He, although

White, was also one of the few teachers, Black or White, who dared visit my neighborhood on Ashmun Street without an escort or body-guard. So, you had to take notice. I also admired Mr. Elwood for not prejudging his students, as some teachers do. As a result, I took a strong liking to Mr. Elwood, and I participated in the marching band, concert band, and stage band, which he directed, until I graduated from Cross. Mr. Elwood became a constant presence in my life.

The first year of band was unforgettable. The entire band consisted of approximately ten students, most of whom had never taken music lessons previously and could barely belt out a note. But Mr. Elwood was determined to make a respectful band out of the group, while also instructing some of the unruly members that they could easily be replaced. He made good on the promise, quickly dispensing of students who clowned during the sessions and found it difficult to focus on the task at hand. Even my sister Gwendolyn, whom I had recommended because she had prior experience playing the clarinet, lasted for only one week. Eventually as some of the members, including myself, gained Mr. Elwood's trust, we told him we would never form a band if he kept getting rid of our recruits. He remained consistent to his standards but softened enough for us to recruit additional members to obtain a band that could march, read notes, and do a respectable job of playing basic tunes. The band would continue to grow after.

I became so busy the first year in high school that I carried a brief case and scheduling book. Fellow students often made fun of me and asked why I carried a briefcase and wore ties to school every day. The briefcase helped me keep all my books and papers together. However, it also communicated that I was serious about what I was doing, and I was. I was on a mission. My calendar book was constantly filled months in advance with various school and social activity appointments. I enjoyed the challenge of learning. I was also careful to try to partake in recreational and other activities as well. And at least one school day and on weekends, I visited my high school girlfriend.

My high school girlfriend and I were close friends. She was unlike any of the other girls I had dated previously. She was ambitious, very caring about the people around her, insightful, and very friendly. She possessed all the good qualities a young man could ask for. We met at Camp Farnam and began dating when I entered Cross. We immensely enjoyed each other's company and had many memorable experiences. I truly felt blessed to have her at my side.

My girlfriend's mother also did everything she could to be supportive of the relationship, including encouraging me in my academic and community pursuits as well as sharing her insights and personal experiences. And I appreciated her for it. However, the father was more guarded in his interactions with me. Still, I became close to the family, whom I genuinely liked and admired, and I remained with this young lady through high school, college, and law school.

When I was not with my girlfriend, I hung out with my buddies. But my friends had become secondary at this point, and they knew it. Although I tremendously enjoyed hanging out with my friends and tried to do so as much as possible, I understood that I had to set priorities, and my studies, work, girlfriend, and friends were my new order of priorities.

Although my childhood friends on Ashmun Street possessed many talents, both academically and otherwise, at the time academics was not their priority, and I understood that. To avoid distraction from my focus, I reduced the amount of time spent with them. This also served to help reduce any influence of my friends in encouraging me to use drugs or alcohol, which were readily available.

When some of my friends began smoking in high school, I refused to participate. This often resulted in further efforts to coax me, without success. Although, on occasion, I drank a beer or two, which lasted a short time, I never found any pleasure in it. This was especially true since I had so many visible examples of how drinking and drugs impacted negatively on the lives of residents in my neighborhood, including two of my friends' parents who were alcoholics. I did not want to become another victim of such indiscretions. Even as a youngster, I was conscious of my reputation and felt a need to keep it clean.

I had also learned a major lesson during the year I resided at the State Receiving Home. The more I visited home, the more I became aware that little changed in my Ashmun Street neighborhood. While progress could be seen in other neighborhoods I visited, in the Dixwell area where I resided, the same people appeared to be doing the same things. The same people were hanging out on the street or starting trouble on the basketball courts or congregating in the trash-filled hallways. The public housing stock was still deteriorating, and no major changes appeared to be on the horizon. Having read many books, including articles about Martin Luther King Jr. and the civil rights movement, I concluded that change only came about when compelled by concerned individuals, and I knew this required positive role models, pressure, and persistence. I strived to be part of the movement for positive change and not an impediment.

I knew there were many residents in my neighborhood who worked and desired good-paying jobs, children who wanted to achieve, and to be associated with people who desired a better life. However, for some reason, these dreams were not publicly espoused, especially if you read the many news articles about the neighborhood. The television news accounts fared no better. The Ashmun and Franklin Street projects were viewed as the outcasts of the city and a place where few residents wanted to make anything positive of their lives. Though this certainly appeared to be the case on the surface, this view was baseless, and I desired to be an example.

Wanting to do my part to combat this outlook, in my second year at Cross, while working as a lifeguard at the Lovell Community Center in the Franklin Street public housing area, I started a volunteer youth jobs program aimed at encouraging the area youth to clean up and maintain the center. The children, not much younger than I, were required to report to me three days a week and complete work assignments, after which they were rewarded with small gifts that I purchased. The purpose of this program was to train the youth in taking responsibility for a task, reporting at an assigned time to perform the task, and observing the positive results of their work. The program worked. I learned that the youth were interested in working. They were willing to take advantage of a work opportunity, and when they themselves were responsible for cleaning up the center, they were more conscientious about keeping the building clean.

I expanded the program to include sponsorship of weekly dances for the youth on Friday evenings as a way of keeping them off the streets and providing constructive activities. These events became known as the Expected Behavior Dance Committee. The weekly dances, with a full buffet for thirty-five cents, became very popular. Parents in the neighborhood volunteered to provide most of the food, without cost. Especially helpful were Ms. Ruth Blango and Ms. Catherine Billups, who always made sure we were fully stocked and provided lots of guidance and encouragement as well.

Ms. Billup's sons, Thomas and Michael, became key organizers with me, as did Ms. Blango's son, Charles, who eventually became a minister and alderperson in New Haven. Both parents yearned for change in the neighborhood. By joining my effort, they not only helped the group gain respect in the Franklin Street neighborhood, but soon youth from Ashmun Street began attending the events, helping lessen the animosity between the rival neighborhoods. When the group expanded to Ashmun Street, Kenny Jenkins became involved, and I changed the group name to Jenkins and Boddie Productions.

In the summer of 1976, the activities were expanded further to include trips for adults and children to amusement parks, such as Riverside Park in Agawam, Massachusetts, and Great Adventures in Jackson, New Jersey. I sponsored the trips for several years before one bus driver learned how young I was. For some reason, he assumed a much older person was sponsoring the trips despite me handing him the payments. After learning of my youth, he complimented me on taking on the project and the behavior of the participants on trips and vowed to be one of our drivers each year after. Gus and my good friend Elise Cuccaro were the first adults from another local town to join the group's efforts. Both were instrumental in helping the group attract residents from their neighborhoods. I had met Elise through Camp Farnam, where I taught her children swimming. Yvette had attended camp along with her brother and sister. We shared a very warm friendship, and when I met her mother Elise, we immediately became friends as well.

Elise resided in West Haven, a town close to New Haven, which at the time could often be an unfriendly environment for Blacks to live or visit. Nevertheless, Elise accepted me as an honorary family member and invited me and my then girlfriend to visit whenever we desired. We visited her house frequently, most of my birthdays as well as holidays. Ironically, Yvette's birthday was the day after mine. I enjoyed not only spending time with the children but debating the news topics of the day with Elise. We had a wonderful time. Elise understood poverty and race relations very well, having transcended poverty and many race issues herself. She was an effective communicator on both subjects, and she showed little tolerance for people who were ignorant or foolish about either subject. And for this, I admired her immensely, because I, too, cherish people who judge others by the content of their character, rather than skin color.

Nevertheless, the first time Elise came with her family on the bus with residents of Ashmun and Franklin Streets, I was terrified, because both communities had a reputation for being unfriendly to Whites. I took a sigh of relief when the bus departed, and I observed that Elise and her family were being treated as if they, too, resided in the neighborhood. In the following years, she brought others from her neighborhood to join us. Elise became a mainstay with the organization and in my life, until her untimely death in a catastrophic automobile accident. And in the process, I lost a wonderful and very dear friend.

In the years after, the organization was incorporated and renamed United Youth Enterprises Inc. United Youth Enterprises Inc. continued to thrive as an all-volunteer organization and grew to serve youth in other states, including New York, New Jersey, Rhode Island, and Massachusetts. During summers, the organization sponsored camping programs at Killam's Point Conference and Retreat Center in Branford, Connecticut. At camp, the youth participated in swimming, fishing, hiking, a buffet dinner, marshmallow roast, late-night storytelling, discussions on doing well in school, and planning early for college. UYE's programs were designed with the intention of providing participants fun activities while encouraging them to pursue academic excellence and become leaders in their communities.

The organization also conducted college and career seminars. The seminars consisted of a panel of speakers who toured high schools in New York City and New Haven, Connecticut, to discuss the college admissions process, myths, and strategies for successful admission and career planning tips for students who did not intend to go to college.

These activities were supplemented with annual summer tours to Washington, DC; Hampton, Virginia; and other cities to educate the youth concerning governmental institutions, local colleges, and leadership. Prior to the attacks on the World Trade Center in New York City, the group was privileged to participate in public tours of the White House, a private meeting with the staff of justices of the US Supreme Court, members of Congress, and frequent tours of the House and Senate Chambers. The group had some wonderfully invaluable experiences, which they have used to their advantage in pursuing a college education and embarking on a variety of careers.

Many of the youth participants of United Youth Enterprises Inc. became staff and board members and continued on to attend Brown, Cornell, University of Pennsylvania, Wesleyan, Northeastern, Howard, Hampton, Morgan, Spellman, Providence College, and so many other universities and to represent a wide variety of careers. Today, they are judges, lawyers, nurses, principals, teachers, and so on. United Youth Enterprises Inc. has received numerous awards for the volunteer efforts of its staff, including two proclamations from the mayor of the city of New Haven and citations from the Nassau County, New York Legislature. In 2000, I also proudly accepted an African American Trailblazer Award from the National Council of Negro Women in New York State honoring my work with United Youth Enterprises Inc.

United Youth Enterprises Inc. has proven to be a real success story evidencing what can happen in communities when concerned individuals come together to create positive change. United Youth Enterprises Inc., to its testament, has been funded solely by concerned individuals and community residents and staffed by volunteers. More importantly, United Youth Enterprises Inc. has made a tremendous contribution in instilling in youth the belief that they can be successful regardless of their family circumstances or economic status. I could never have predicted that so much would come from my simple gesture to create this organization to uplift the community while a sophomore in high school.

My sophomore year at Cross, Gwendolyn and I shared a chemistry class taught by Mr. Blosveren, a very serious-looking teacher with round wire-rim glasses. He was as serious as he appeared. Mr. Blosveren did not tolerate any nonsense. So, when Gwendolyn and I took the chemistry class together, she became a more serious student than she had been the previous year. I added to the pressure by challenging her to see who could get the best chemistry grade. We both received good grades. She proved a tough competitor, but I won with the better final grade by a half point. In the process, I learned just how smart my sister really is. She gained my full respect and admiration. Gwendolyn eventually continued on to attend and graduate from college while raising two children and embarked on a career as a registered nurse.

While giving major focus to my high school academic studies sophomore year, I also became a student peer counselor. The peer counseling program was an experiment conducted by a graduate student at Yale while seeking his PhD. When told about the plan for the program, I was extremely excited about participating. I thought I could be productive in offering moral, social, and educational advice to fellow students and was honored to be asked to participate.

I was equally thrilled when I met the graduate student and was selected for the project. Although the gentleman's name now escapes me, I will never forget the impression he made on me. He was a very tall Black man, about the height of Wilt Chamberlain, one of my favorite basketball players at the time. As impressed as I was about his size, I was equally impressed by the fact that he attended Yale and was a doctoral candidate in psychology no less. My impoverished Ashmun Street neighborhood bordered the Yale campus, and I visited the campus often. I knew that many of the country's best and brightest students attended Yale. Consequently, I wanted to soak up everything this man had to offer.

The students selected for the project met with him and a teacher advisor for several training sessions. Then we were set free to begin counseling a preselected group of students. We reported our progress at regularly scheduled weekly meetings with our advisors. I enjoyed the experience immensely. I learned that I really enjoyed helping people. I gained a lot of insight from listening to the problems of students, who were mostly freshman, and in providing advice to them about how to do well academically and avoid the all too frequent pressures of using drugs, alcohol, and getting into trouble with girls. In the process, the group learned that students similar in age were more inclined to take the advice of other students. We were very successful in helping students enhance their study skills and stay out of trouble. Unfortunately, the project ended after one year.

During my involvement with this project, I met Ms. Maryellen Mininberg, a demanding and wise teacher who taught English to some of the most academically talented students at Cross. I never took her class because I was not very excited about reading the large numbers of books she required. Nonetheless, I knew she was a committed teacher and a master in her field. After taking the SATs and not performing well, I sought her advice. She agreed to assist me in preparing to retake the test but only if I stayed after school several days weekly and agreed to continue studying during the summer. It was a tough request, but I accepted.

I studied numerous workbooks with her assistance and completed the required exercises. The entire summer, Ms. Mininberg showed tremendous dedication working with me on my vocabulary and grammar on her personal time, without compensation. I remain truly grateful for her assistance. Unfortunately, the retake of the test did not improve my scores. But I was determined not to let this stop me. I was on a mission.

I searched every available resource, and a friend pointed me to a professor at Yale University to coach me. Although I was nervous about going to see someone of such stature, I made an appointment with the secretary and went to see him. The gentleman was a very distinguished-looking Black man, and unknown to him, this would be my first visit inside Yale Law School by invitation. All times prior, I and my friends had simply used the school as a shortcut to get home.

The professor made me feel comfortable immediately by asking me to tell him a little about myself, my background, and my goals. I spoke eloquently about my childhood growing up on Ashmun Street, my determination to succeed, and my desire to attend an Ivy League School and become a doctor. At that time, I wanted to become a doctor and help heal the afflictions that poor people suffered, mentally and physically.

I had no idea I would eventually become a lawyer. Nor was I aware at the time that my mother was a legal celebrity, having been the lead plaintiff in a widely renowned divorce case in the US Supreme Court known as *Boddie v. State of Connecticut*. In *Boddie*, a group of welfare recipients in Connecticut found their efforts at obtaining a divorce encumbered with the necessity to pay court fees. After their efforts to obtain a waiver of the fees failed, they filed a lawsuit, arguing, in effect, that their due process rights to divorce were violated by virtue of the fees hindering their access to the courts for the purpose of obtaining a divorce. The Connecticut courts denied them the relief sought. On appeal, the US Supreme Court reversed the Connecticut court's determination. In doing so, the US Supreme Court held divorce is a fundamental right guaranteed by the US Constitution, and such right may not be impeded by virtue of such fees, thus propelling the concept and widespread use of fee waivers in civil cases throughout the United States.

Ironically, this case was one of the first cases filed by the Legal Services Corporation office in my neighborhood, then known as Dixwell Legal Rights, where I would also eventually work while attending college. However, my mother and I would not learn of her celebrity status until my brother David entered Texas Southern Law School, which ironically was a school initially developed to forestall integration of Texas University Law School after the decision in another famous US Supreme Court case, *Sweatt v. Painter*. David told my mother about the importance of the case after his law school buddies joked about our mother "starting trouble in Connecticut." It would be the first time she and I learned the case was of national prominence and taught in law schools throughout the country.

Therefore, I missed the opportunity to share this information with the professor. Still, he was impressed with my determination and told me that although he had serious doubts as to whether I could attend Yale because of its strong reliance on SAT scores, it was possible another Ivy League School would accept me, and he would do everything to help. When we next met, he provided me all the specifics regarding what was needed to present a successful application, including how to explain the fact that I did not test well on the SAT.

Around this time, I also became involved with the Black Coalition of Greater New Haven. The Black Coalition was one of New Haven's foremost and respected civil rights organizations. Led by Rev. Dr. Jimmy E. Jones, executive director, the organization was the annual sponsor of the city-wide Black Expo and at the forefront of mostly every civil rights issue that involved people of African descent in the Greater New Haven area.

Rev. Dr. Robert Jones, another good friend—formerly of the Fair Haven Parents' Ministry, where I previously lived—and then director of the Lovell Community Center in Fair Haven, had introduced me to Jimmy Jones (of no relationship) during one of his visits to the Lovell Community Center. Unknown to me then, Robert Jones and Jimmy Jones had been roommates while attending Yale Divinity School. Robert told Jimmy about my successful work with children at Lovell Community Center and my determination to succeed. Jimmy responded by inviting me to become a member of the Black Expo Planning Committee. I was deeply honored by the request, although I did not think I had enough time to include another activity in my schedule. However, this was an opportunity I could not refuse, to work with an organization at the center of advocating on issues of concern to Black residents of the Greater New Haven area and as a member of the committee helping plan one of the most significant events in the New Haven Community, the annual Black Expo.

The committee met weekly. I was the only high school student on the committee, which consisted of corporate leaders and numerous big-name community leaders, including Jimmy Jones, Emma Jones, Ed Grant of the Freddy Fixer Parade Committee, Cliff Bush of the United Illuminating Company, and others. At first, I was a little intimidated by the impressive array of adults, who were very accomplished in their fields and well-known in the community, but I eventually grew accustomed to being in their presence.

My volunteer work on the committee gave me an invaluable opportunity to hone my organizational skills as we planned the details of each event, ranging from theme and activities to facilities and contracting, budgeting, public relations, and security. I also received immeasurable experience from observing how Jimmy Jones managed the staff. Jimmy and Emma would eventually become my mentors and close personal friends.

With the knowledge and experience, I gained during my sophomore year at Cross, I felt truly prepared to make even greater achievements when I entered my junior year, and I knew I had to make the best of it because it would be my last opportunity to demonstrate and hone my skills before the college applications were due.

I began my junior year by enrolling in some of the most challenging courses, including physics and sociology. I worked even harder on my studies and sought to learn everything I could. While focusing on my studies, I continued participating in a variety of school activities, including three bands, president of the student council, yearbook editor, the honor society, and the science fiction club, among others. I also worked after school and was involved in a wide variety of community activities. As a result, there was little room for error in managing my time.

I rarely spent time at home, except to sleep. I did not arrive at home until late at night, instead doing most of my studying before the start of my shift at work and at home late at night if I did not complete my assignments prior to arriving home. However, since I did not cherish doing homework late at night, I did everything possible to try to complete the work before arriving home. This allowed me to enhance my study techniques, learning creative ways to retain large amounts of information. And the benefits were apparent by the excellent grades I received.

My junior year at Cross, Ms. Mininberg approached me about reestablishing a student council at Cross. Cross had a student council several years before I arrived, but it had become extinct. I agreed to work with her on the project. We met weekly for several months writing, reviewing, and debating the advantages and disadvantages of each clause in the proposed constitution and bylaws of the student council we were seeking to develop. We then solicited the entire school for interested students. Among that first group, the officers were voted upon. I was elected to serve as president and immediately created an ambitious agenda of items to address, with input from the student body.

The student council sponsored blood drives, school spirit days, tackled issues of books in the library, decorum in the cafeteria, Black history classes, and a host of other topics. The student council became an effective advocacy organization at Cross. Student interest in the council was high after the first year. In subsequent years, representatives from each class, freshman, sophomore, junior, and senior, were required to campaign to serve on the student council. I was proudly reelected as president and saw this as a mandate that I was headed in the right direction.

Recognizing the success and interest of the students and the leadership of the student council, the school principal Robert Conte introduced me to Dr. Gerald Tirozzi, then superintendent of New Haven Public Schools. Mr. Conte joked with Dr. Tirozzi about me being a young man on the move who kept him on his toes. At the time, I wasn't sure what to make of this comment, but it impressed Gerald Tirozzi, and he offered to be of assistance to me in any way he could. He also invited the student council presidents in the city to meet with him regularly to keep him abreast of current issues. Dr. Tirozzi and I have been friends ever since.

In the interim, Mr. Conte tapped me to replace him doing the daily announcements on the school public address system. I was extremely impressed with his confidence in me and learned to handle the task well. The first week I was very nervous about speaking to the entire school over the public address system. However, Ms. Mininberg assisted me with intonation and previewed the messages for me. This gave me additional confidence, and soon after I was on my own. Each morning when I arrived, I was handed a bunch of announcements to read. I added some comments to my satisfaction and delivered them over the public address system. Before long, students who previously talked throughout the announcements told me that they were listening in each day to hear my new tidbits. I mastered the technique of grabbing their attention by starting each presentation with "Good morning, Wilburs" and ending with a positive point about the day ahead. I loved the job.

In contrast, my work as student council president was not always glorious, but it was very rewarding. I was looked upon to quell issues before they got out of hand. Such was the case when Black students at Cross thought the school was trying to terminate the Black history teacher along with all Black history classes. I inquired and was told this was not the case. Nevertheless, the rumor persisted and was creating a lot of uneasiness among the students at Cross, which at the time was predominantly White.

During this rocky period, I was asked by the school to meet with a gentleman at the Center for Advocacy, Research and Planning (CARP) to answer some questions about this. I met with Fleming Norcott Jr., who was then the executive director of CARP, a civil rights research, advocacy, and litigation organization. This very intelligent-looking Black man, whom I would only later learn was an attorney, asked me a series of innocuous questions about race relations at Cross. Although I was never sure what direction the questions were headed, I answered them as best I could.

When I finished, he told me if ever I needed assistance with any matters relating to school, I could come see him. When I returned to school, I was questioned about the subject matter of our conversation. Consequently, although I never really knew what that CARP visit was all about, I did understand that the school did not want to make trouble with Mr. Norcott. I stayed in contact with and often visited him in court after he became a judge. I was also right about my inclination that he was not a man to tinker with. Fleming Norcott went on to serve as the first Black judge of the Connecticut Supreme Court, the highest court in the state.

In addition to my role as president of the student council, I continued to play the trombone in all three bands conducted by Mr. Elwood. As previously indicated, when I arrived at Cross my freshman year, the band consisted of ten people, who were not very good musicians. However, Mr. Elwood remained determined to build a first-class band from the ground up. His hard work and all the students' efforts really began to pay off my junior year. Students began auditioning for band, and those who were not willing to follow the rules were terminated. Band truly became an enjoyable experience.

The concert band played at school concerts, as well as city-wide events. The stage band played funky pop music for special events at school and away, and the marching band marched in parades. I enjoyed playing with all the bands. However, I especially enjoyed the stage band with the electric guitars. The stage band was always arranged professionally with an orchestra type of format, and we belted out the hits of the day, Barry White, Kool & the Gang, Chicago, and others. I truly enjoyed the music and the response we got from the students. Whenever the stage band played, the audiences were whipped into a frenzy, and we usually left them begging for more.

Although previously I had been considered a nerd, by junior year my talents were showcased, and more students were beginning to see me for who I really was. As a result, I became very popular and gained wide recognition, not only with the students but also with the teachers. Still, I carried my weight in a dignified manner and was never boastful. With my newfound popularity, I was invited to join countless school organizations and events in and outside of school. I accepted some, including yearbook editor, and declined others, as my focus remained to gain admission to an Ivy League school.

Utilizing all the information gathered from my various sources, at the end of my junior year, I sent out letters requesting applications from nearly twenty schools. I selected approximately twelve schools to apply to, including Brown, Yale, and Harvard. I grouped the schools in three tiers: four dream schools, a second group of less difficult schools, and a third group of schools I considered to be my "guarantee" schools. It was my hope and desire that this strategic approach would insure my admission to one or more colleges.

Another challenge was presented when I retook the SAT my senior year and failed to improve my scores. Many people who had previously encouraged me began to question whether I could gain admission to an Ivy League School. This surprised me a great deal. I was dismayed that they accepted the SAT results at face value hook, line, and sinker.

I made every effort to explain that I did not perform well on standardized tests, but my comments mostly fell on deaf ears. As a result, I knew it was critical that I prove myself and minimize the effect and impact of their negativity on me.

Despite this setback, my friend at Yale remained encouraged and advised me to gather a team of people who would advocate favorably for me. However, the catch was these people had to feel comfortable not only discussing my success but also articulating the fact that the SAT results were not reflective of my abilities. Initially, my thoughts were where would I find such people. But soon after, I reflected to having addressed this issue previously at Becket Academy and prevailing against similar opposition.

I accepted the offer of a friend at the Urban League to coach me in writing, review my essays, and provide me application fee assistance. I next went to speak with my previous math teacher Saundra Stephenson to explain my dilemma and exactly what I needed her and other teachers to do. I virtually dictated specific language to her and asked if she was comfortable writing a recommendation. To my surprise and elation, she told me it was not a dilemma at all. She not only felt comfortable doing it, but indicated I deserved it, and if any other teacher I approached did not feel comfortable doing it, I should not have them write for me. She also agreed to lead my team of supporters and monitor the efforts. The strategy worked flawlessly, except for one teacher and my guidance counselor.

An English teacher complained about me privately to scuttle my plans, although she, too, had previously given me a good grade. My guidance counselor too, although publicly supporting me, came up with many excuses to delay writing my recommendations and mailing the grades. When I finally confronted him in a friendly conversation, he told me that he was not entirely comfortable because his son, who was also graduating, was smart and attending a less well-known college, and he was uncomfortable pushing me for such prestigious schools that I probably would not get into.

I was both surprised and insulted to hear my counselor, who previously never had anything negative to say about me, share such comments. But I did everything not to let him know it. Yet I appreciated his honesty and frankness because it foretold what I was up against. Instead of responding with anger, I reasoned with him, reminding him of my consistent honor grades, my successful involvement with numerous school clubs, including the student council, the neighborhood I grew up in, and my desire to improve my life. I also compared myself to another student at the school who had performed well academically and on the SAT but did not demonstrate the same leadership skills and encouraged that he not let his personal beliefs stand in the path of my goals. I beckoned, what if I was right? He reluctantly agreed that I should have the chance. Still, I monitored him closely, nearly every day, until I was sure all my recommendations were completed and mailed.

In the interim, I attended a Brown University recruitment event in New Haven where I met Dave Zucconi, a consummate alumni recruiter. He was as skilled as any professional salesman and a wonderful person. Dave sold me on Brown over all the other schools and encouraged me to visit the campus to see for myself. The story Dave shared with the audience at the recruitment event about all the great things at Brown sounded almost too good to be true. Thus, I could not wait to see for myself. When I visited Brown, I was not disappointed. I was very impressed with the curriculum, the friendliness of the students, and the faculty's emphasis on undergraduate education. When the letter of acceptance from Brown arrived in April, I was ecstatic. Not only was I accepted to Brown, I received a full scholarship.

The day after receiving notice of my admission to Brown, I could not wait to seek out Ms. Stephenson to share the good news and thank her for the support. Her hard work and commitment both comforted me and helped make a world of difference in my life. Although Ms. Stephenson usually arrived in her classroom early, that day I had a problem locating her, so I told my guidance counselor first. When I told my guidance counselor, he was so happy you would have thought he won the lottery. He was overjoyed that he relented to my request and was vindicated in doing so. Ms. Stephenson and Ms. Mininberg also were very happy to hear the news.

Later that day, I learned that Cross made history. Brown diverted from its past practices of accepting one student annually from my school and accepted two. I was bursting with joy. I was happy not only for myself but also for the other student, Shelly Hare. I had always admired Shelly Hare and her family. Her mom had been my gym teacher many years earlier at Winchester School, and Shelly and I had maintained a fondness for each other since.

With my admission to Brown settled, I felt vindicated for my zealous advocacy regarding the need for schools to focus on grades, class standing, leadership, and other markers of success in addition to standardized test scores. I felt strongly then, as I do now, that many colleges would surely recognize that scores on a standardized test alone cannot determine success in college in every case. So, the real question was, Would the school be willing to take a chance on me? Brown heeded the message, and I was determined to repay the favor. I knew the real test would lie ahead in my success or failure as a student at Brown. Yet I was more determined than ever to take advantage of this opportunity. It was an opportunity that I had earnestly desired and prayed for.

The remainder of my senior year, I continued to pursue my studies diligently to earn as many A grades as possible. I taught swimming at the YWCA on Saturdays and at the Boys and Girls' Clubs Monday through Friday, continued my term as student council president, played trombone in the band, and participated in numerous other extracurricular activities. When June arrived, I graduated from Cross with high honors and received numerous awards. Most memorable among them was my inclusion in the worldwide publication *Who's Who Among American High School Students* and my classmates voting me "Done Most for Class." Ironically, my classmates also voted me "Most Likely to Succeed," but I was denied this award because the school thought it would be unfair to recognize me in two categories. As the year wound down, Shelly and I began to plot our next steps at Brown. At the time, we had both planned to pursue a career in medicine and take some of the same courses. We also issued a challenge to each other to graduate from Brown together.

We graduated high school on my birthday, June 14, 1977, in historic Woolsey Hall on the Yale University campus. Woolsey Hall was located just several blocks from the Ashmun Street projects in which I resided. On the night of the graduation, I walked to the hall with several friends as we reflected on how quickly the years passed, contemplated our futures, and how drastically our lives would change. Since I was in the band, upon arrival, I took my place in the pit area that separated the first row of seats and the stage. From my seat, I was able to appreciate the huge hall in all its grandeur. The view from my seat was spectacular and undoubtedly the best in the hall apart from the people who sat on the stage. I warmed my trombone and waited for the hall to fill. Unlike my past visits to Woolsey Hall where I played for other graduations, this time I felt a special sense of pride, since it was now my chance to play for my own graduation and that of my beloved senior classmates.

As the graduates lined up, the band belted out "Pomp and Circumstances." The sound of our instruments filled the hall wonderfully and as it never had before. After the graduates filled their seats, loud applause erupted. The band played a selection in the program. This time, like no other, all the trombone players were graduating, so we were given the opportunity to do a trombone solo. We played like never before to a great response by the audience.

The rewarding of diplomas prompted more loud applause as each student's name was announced and we walked to the stage to receive our diplomas. This was a united class, and each student took satisfaction in the success of others. I was elated since this was exactly the goal I, as president of the student council, and the class president Keith Minore, had set out to achieve. It clearly reflected the unity and efforts of the class throughout the year.

When my name was called and I approached the stage to receive my diploma, another loud roar erupted as I was thanked for all my work on behalf of the class. I was gracious in my response yet truly grateful for the support and cooperation my classmates demonstrated our entire four years at Cross. And deep within me, at that moment, I knew how much I would miss my fellow classmates.

At the end of the graduation program, the band played the graduation recession song. This time the recession seemed like no other. It became apparent to me that this would be the last time I would ever play the recession in the Cross band. There would be no next year. I wanted the song to last forever. And as the group of graduates grew smaller exiting the hall, reality set in that I now had to move on to the next challenge.

As is customary, the band left the hall last. I said my goodbyes to each band member and thanked Mr. Elwood for all his support. I then left the hall to walk home with some of my friends. As soon as I left the hall and entered Ashmun Street, the excitement of being in such a great hall and on the campus of such a great institution as Yale struck me as it never had before, when I thought about the life of poverty I had lived in the projects for so many years just down the street. At this moment, there was no doubt I was a ready to leave New Haven to begin my journey toward a new life and new beginnings at Brown.

That summer, I returned to visit Brown for what was commonly referred to as Third World Weekend. This was a weekend program designed to provide newly admitted students of color, as we were referred to, an opportunity to meet each other prior to the start of school and to learn what services were available to assist in our academic success. During the weekend, I met students of color from across the country and of vastly different economic status and social environments than I had been accustomed. This would be the first time I met very wealthy Black people, at least to my knowledge. However, everyone expressed commitment to one goal—graduating from Brown and helping each other do so together. As a result, there was a remarkable feeling of unity among us when the weekend was over, and I left the campus feeling relaxed and fully prepared to return in September.

CHAPTER 5

Reggie Blossoms at Brown

When I arrived at Brown in September 1977, I was elated to learn that my roommate was David Makkers, a very intelligent and gentlemanly Black man I had met at Third World Weekend. David grew up in Providence and attended private school prior to attending Brown. I desired to learn more about Providence, and he could show me around. He was also neat, which was a big issue for me. David strongly believed in God and prayer. And no doubt, I knew that it was only by the grace of God that I had arrived at this point in my life, and I was not about to deny that. Therefore, David and I often attended church together with his mother and father.

I truly admired David's parents. I fell in love with them the first time we met. This was a rare event for me. David's parents, although living in the North, had very warm Southern charm. They told me immediately since I was their son's roommate, we must support each other in being successful and they would do whatever they could to help. They continued, "Whenever David comes home, you are welcome to come with him and consider yourself our adopted son." How can anyone refuse nice people like that, who not only articulated these words but followed through on every promise? I truly came to feel like I had another family in Providence and often visited their home, even if for nothing more than good conversation. Each time I visited, I was made to feel so welcome it was hard to leave. David's parents spent countless hours talking to me about the history of Providence, the neighborhoods, Brown, the history of Blacks in Providence, and the political landscape. They were wonderful lessons, all delivered for free and with loving intensity. This made me want to succeed even more to make them as well as my mother and friends proud.

Although we enjoyed each other's company immensely, David and I rarely spent much time together other than in the room and on weekends because he was an engineering major and I was pursuing premedical studies. Engineering majors had intensive course schedules, and most had little time to spare outside their studies.

My first-year courses at Brown included biology, calculus, English, and others. I was excited about being a premedical student and one step closer to becoming a doctor. I especially enjoyed the labs affiliated with the biology courses. This allowed me to develop a hands-on approach to science, which enhanced my retention of the lessons. The introduction to biology class was, however, a real awakening. The class was filled with mostly premedical students and biology majors. Consequently, the class was held in a huge lecture hall with hundreds of students and informally referred to as the weed-out class, intended to weed out all but the strongest students. Unlike high school, no attendance was taken, and if you did not show up, no one would notice. However, students were responsible for mastering the material in both the lecture and laboratory section of the class.

This was a real test for the brightest of students, because a premium was placed on working together in groups to share information, assisting each other in understanding different concepts, and requesting assistance from instructors when appropriate. I made use of every avenue and opportunity available to me and passed the course.

I passed my other courses the first year as well, but my first-year college calculus course provided a special challenge. The course was taught by Professor Loobis. Mr. Loobis was an uncharacteristically bald man who appeared extremely smart. He entered the class with a strict business attitude and left with the same. There was never room for jokes.

Professor Loobis wrote on multiple boards at a time, and very quickly. You could easily get lost if you could not decipher his writing or the direction of the notes on the boards. Still, it was best to hold questions, unless you desired to advertise to the entire class that your high school math course might have been somewhat inadequate to prepare you for Brown. Although I recognized many of the concepts thanks to my math teachers at Cross, I had problems keeping up with the quickened pace and the theory.

After becoming frustrated and determining that passing was more important than pride, I informed Professor Loobis of my problem and was surprised that he not only recommended and located a tutor for me, he personally guided me to make sure I passed. In the process, despite his intimidating appearance, I learned that he was a very wonderful, caring person. This made me less hesitant in asking questions of other professors and less judging of the extent to which they might be helpful to me. To my delight, I passed both Calculus 9 and 10.

I thoroughly enjoyed my first year at Brown and was certain by the end of the year that I had chosen the right school. The professors were very committed to teaching undergraduate students and to providing them as much access to experts in different disciplines as graduate students. I was pleased that Brown placed special emphasis on teaching undergraduates, as advertised. The special curriculum at Brown, often referred to as the new curriculum, also allowed students to experiment by taking courses in a varied assortment of areas without receiving a letter grade. Instead, students had the option of taking certain courses ABC/no credit or obtaining a satisfactory / no credit. Brown did not award Ds. Therefore, students who scored below C received a grade of NC, known as no credit.

The satisfactory/no credit option was deceptive, even if it encouraged exploration. Very often work in mandatory S/NC classes was more demanding than other classes simply because they were mandatory S/NC classes. Therefore, the more informed students checked concerning these matters prior to enrolling in the S/NC courses.

I was also pleased to learn that Brown was very committed to seeing that every student succeeded academically and did all it could to make services available to insure this outcome. At the same time, unlike many other schools, Brown actively encouraged students to develop socially as well as academically. Therefore, participation in extracurricular activities was strongly encouraged.

I found most students and alumni at Brown to be friendly, just as Dave Zucconi had represented to me. Most Brown students and alumni were unlike the elitist snobbish types I had often met from some other Ivy League Schools. In contrast, Brown students and alumni were often willing to talk and help. There was an excitement about being affiliated with Brown that even spilled over to the road. Even in rush hour traffic, fellow "Brunonians" often honked to say hello after seeing my Brown sticker on the car window. It exuded a wonderful feeling about Brown as an institution.

In contrast, the cultural and economic divide at Brown was truly an awakening experience for me. I had never met such large numbers of wealthy people before entering Brown. I had occasionally met people who did not have a real understanding of Black culture or the struggle of Blacks in America. However, for the first time, at Brown I also met some Black people who appeared to be unfamiliar with these issues. This was troubling to me because of the well-known history of progress through struggle, which resulted in the many achievements of Blacks in America. And if people at Ivy League Schools, who were regarded to be the future leaders of our country, were lackadaisical about the status and continuing need for progress on this front, I wondered about the future.

Consequently, whenever an opportunity presented itself, I reminded my friends and colleagues about the realities outside the Brown campus. I often used myself as an example, to remind them that my experience was not atypical, and I did not arrive at Brown easily, and there were many more people, both poor Whites and Blacks, that if given the opportunity, could excel as I had.

At Brown, social discourse was a regular event, whether the discussions were formal or informal. I would use the opportunity to remind people that although many students at Brown were from private schools, there are many people who cannot afford to go to private schools and would do just as well at an Ivy League School. I also expressed that, although I grew up in low-income housing projects, there were many people in the projects who were just as intelligent who might never get the opportunities I received. Therefore, their talents would not be recognized, although if given the chance they, too, could attend and succeed at an Ivy League School.

My favorite was discussing the SAT scores because all too many students felt that achieving high marks on the SAT entitled them to superior status. For these people, I emphasized that although I was proud of the fact that they performed well on the SAT, the SAT did not test motivation. I also reminded them that no one is concerned with the scores of people who are successful. Many of us know very successful people. Can you imagine querying them about their standardized test scores? Not only would it be irrelevant and unnecessary but an insult as well.

I will never forget the day I had a discussion with a member of the Brown Corporation on this issue. I met the gentlemen on the street near the Brown campus. I had developed the habit of saying hello to mostly everyone when I crossed his path. It is an old habit, one I had gotten used to in high school. This brisk morning, I said hello to a stranger. He was surprised and stopped to ask my name. One question led to another, and before long we were engaged in a lengthy conversation about where I grew up, my high school, how I arrived at Brown, what excited me about Brown, my plans for the future, my work with youth, and the SAT exams.

Intending to congratulate me, he told me that it was wonderful that I had overcome such obstacles and still arrived at Brown. Not knowing who he was at the time, I took a big leap and told him how thankful I was that Brown had given me such an opportunity, but there were thousands of other Blacks like me who probably would never receive this opportunity. He became very interested in hearing more and told me he was a member of the Brown Corporation and invited me to a lacrosse game with his family the next day so we could talk. I was pleased that his interest and openness to this issue was aroused. And in listening to me, he offered inspiration. Although I was unable to find the time to attend the game and continue our conversation, I never shied away again about discussing the deficiencies of the test.

I also used other opportunities to remind my friends at Brown of the continuing need for progress, both racially and culturally. A vivid example was the complaint of Black students on campus of being frequently followed or stopped by the campus police and questioned. Whenever I heard these complaints, I took the opportunity to remind students that as uncomfortable as this felt and as wrong as it might be to assume that because of our color we were not Brown students, according to many news outlets, this behavior was being replicated in many communities across the country and should not be tolerated, wherever it occurred.

I also reminded them that just as many Blacks on campus were referring to Providence residents as townies, we, too, were often being viewed in a like manner, as if we did not belong to the Brown community or were otherwise suspect. Therefore, I encouraged that we not refer to our fellow brothers and sisters in a like manner. And to further emphasize the point, I spent a great deal of time bringing community residents to campus to demonstrate that they were not much different.

The first of these projects was the Saturday Enrichment Tutorial Program (SETP).

SETP was a Saturday morning tutorial program run by Brown students out of the Third World Center. The program was directed at enhancing the academic skills of minority youngsters, ages six to twelve, all of which resided in impoverished neighborhoods. I joined the program my sophomore year, along with nearly ten other Brown students. We tutored students in mathematics and English on Saturday mornings and took the students on monthly trips to different cities. This allowed us to both encourage the students academically while mentoring them. It was a welcome relief from my studies and provided me an invaluable opportunity to give back to young people who were growing up in neighborhoods like mine. I would eventually become the coordinator for the program.

Working as a volunteer at the John Hope Settlement House in Providence, I also founded the Community Information Group. There, I met weekly with a group of high school students from a predominantly Black neighborhood to discuss major events in the community, locally and nationally, and took them on trips to different cities to observe the progress, or lack thereof. I frequently brought the youth to Brown so they could become familiar with a college campus and began thinking about college as a personal goal. After one of the administrators at the John Hope Settlement House objected to the group traveling, I decided to make the group an independent organization to preserve its integrity, because travel was a significant part of the experience. I was seeking to expose these young people to neighborhoods other than their own to expand their experience and dreams and refused to let bureaucracy stand in the way.

Most of the parents in the community gave me strong support, and the program flourished. The group visited numerous states, including Massachusetts, New Jersey, and Connecticut. They also participated in a Brown radio talk show to discuss their experiences and encourage other youths. I have remained in touch with several of these youth since. Among them, Rochelle Ives, currently works in the Brown University gifts office. Brian Briggs is a retired sergeant major in the army and is married to Robin Briggs, another former member of the group. Marilyn Hareld went on to graduate from the University of Pennsylvania, and Yalta Sanders is employed as a supervisor with a major telecommunications company.

Near the conclusion of my second year at Brown, I began seriously questioning whether I really wanted to become a doctor. I thought with money and intellect I could not only help heal people but make positive change in the world socially and politically. However, I began realizing that the issues of most interest to me, fighting poverty, improving housing conditions, and addressing discrimination in education and employment, were more compatible with being a lawyer. As a result, I began reading more politically conscious books and talking to professionals in both areas to resolve my internal conflict. The fact that many of my friends in New Haven were already calling me Dr. Boddie made the decision more difficult, because I knew they were relying on me to deliver. Likewise, at the time, my older brother David was already attending law school at Texas Southern University, and I did not want to walk in his shadow.

I pondered my decision whether to change from premed to prelaw for a long time and decided to make the decision after returning from summer break. However, after returning from summer vacation, I found I had not progressed much further in making the decision, so I enrolled in chemistry and some other premedical requirements. I completed the semester. When I returned from the next semester break, I could no longer wait in making the determination. This would also be my final opportunity without creating a situation where I had to take additional classes to graduate on time if I changed majors. Therefore, I decided to visit Reverend Small, an assistant chaplain on campus. He was very friendly and a wonderful person to know. We had met previously and seemed to like each other. However, most important, he was known for speaking his mind regardless of the topic, so I believed that I could trust him to give me a truthful answer.

On the day I met with Reverend Small to discuss this matter, it seemed like the end of the world as I had once come to know it. But I had to confront this issue once and for all.

It was invading all my thoughts and sleep. When I entered Reverend Small's office, he asked what I needed that required such urgency. I explained my situation and concerns in a frank manner. He listened politely and asked whether I was ready to make the decision. I responded affirmatively. He said, "I am going to ask you only two questions." I thought to myself, *What makes him think he can resolve such a serious matter with just two questions?* Nonetheless, I responded, "Okay." He then stated, "Why do you want to be a doctor?" I stuttered and muttered a response. He then asked, "Why do you want to be a lawyer?" I responded succinctly and eloquently about helping people in need, fighting injustice in employment, education, housing, and so on. He then responded, "You already made your decision." I said, "What?" with astonishment. He said, "It should be obvious you were able to tell me in detail why you want to be a lawyer but not the same manner when asked about being a doctor." I thanked him for his assistance and never looked back.

I changed my major from biology to psychology. I have always loved studying the behavior of people and yearned to know a great deal more. However, since Brown's psychology program at that time was more laboratory focused than clinical, I decided to pursue an independent concentration in psychology. This is significant for two reasons.

First, because if I had not attended Brown, which had no required primary courses for enrolled students, unlike most other schools, I would not have been able to change concentration midstream without risk of graduating late. Second, Brown's curriculum provided for independent study, thus permitting students to devise their own discipline of study, with approval of the school curriculum committee.

After being unable to locate an already approved independent study project that met my interests, I drafted a proposal for an urban psychology major. This course of study encompassed a mixture of psychology, sociology, and urban studies courses directed at analyzing and understanding the social, psychological, and housing pressures on city residents. My proposal was approved. And I began my new course of study immediately. I thoroughly enjoyed the experience and did well academically.

One of my classes led me to work at Rhode Island Legal Services, in downtown Providence, where I represented tenants at administrative hearings in housing cases and wrote memos for lawyers. I also wrote two papers, "Tenant Organizing in Providence" and "Public Housing in Providence," which were novel at the time and used by lawyers at Rhode Island Legal Services for strategy purposes. I remained at Rhode Island Legal Services for two years and in the process met some wonderful people, including John Dineen, Gary Powers, Robert Sable, Rogerie Thompson, and Robert Barge, the current executive director, who also served as one of my mentors. Each became my friend and contributed to my development immensely.

Another of my classes in education led me to a project studying magnet schools in Providence. The project, performed in concert with a group of Brown students, focused on three public high schools. My team studied the magnet program at Central High School. At that time, magnet programs were viewed as the alternative to mandatory busing to integrate schools. Each school was designed with a special curriculum to attract students on a voluntary basis. My team goal was to determine whether the programs were effective in integrating the schools. We found that magnet schools served their designed purpose of attracting integrated groups to the schools, but the integration terminated at the front door. Once inside, the students were racially grouped for classes, which led to stark racial distinctions, not only at Central but the other schools the class studied as well. The effective result was that college-bound advance classes were almost entirely White, while Blacks occupied the remainder.

However, then Arthur Zarrella served as the principal of Central High School. Mr. Zarrella, an Italian, shared that he was tired of his students thinking they were second class compared to the students at the predominantly White Classical High School next door. After receiving my team report, instead of making excuses, he challenged me to use my resources at Brown to do whatever I could to help. I accepted his challenge and wrote a proposal for the Central High School College Preparatory Program. I recruited two other Brown students to join me, one of which was a graduate student. Each week, we visited English classes at the school to encourage the students to attend college and assisted them in completing and filing their college and financial aid applications.

We did not want to rely on the guidance counselors to do the job, since our goal was to change the status quo. We also did not want any single guidance counselor to be able to trump our efforts, particularly considering my experience at Cross. However, I spoke to the guidance counselors about the program and requested their cooperation. They agreed to cooperate, but some honestly told us they felt insulted we did not use them instead of the English teachers to channel our program. Well, they obviously got the point. If this encouraged them to work harder because we were looking over their shoulders, it was an effective tool.

That is exactly what happened. College applications at the school spiked, and we saw many students who knew nothing about college being educated about them, applying, and getting in. We also took notice that historically Black colleges were the most willing to take chances on these young people. As a result, most of the students who desired to attend college gained admission to at least two schools. We made a difference. The principal thanked us, and the success of the program became the subject of a front-page story in the Brown campus newspaper and a feature article in the *Providence Journal* newspaper.

As a result of our success, the program also got Brown University's attention, and Brown again began looking at and enrolling students from Providence public schools. Prior to graduation, the Brown admissions office invited me to interview for a vacancy for an admissions officer position. I was honored by the invitation and interested, but I respectfully declined since I desired to attend law school. Nevertheless, I was very pleased that I was able to make a difference.

Recently, I read an article in the *Brown Alumni Magazine* about a student of African descent that attended Central High School and went on to graduate from Brown and returned to the high school to teach. My heart burst with joy. Although I do not know whether she was a student at Central when the program was in place, clearly the school is still reaping the benefits desired—that public school students, even at Central, are given serious consideration for admission to Brown. By empowering students who attend schools in Providence, Brown is also empowering the local citizenry and uplifting their communities. This is good for Brown and good for Providence.

Through my work in the Providence community, I learned that the residents are a very friendly and close-knit group. They are among the friendliest people I have ever met in any city. Thus, my experience in reaching out to the residents of Providence, in all my different capacities, was extremely fulfilling and rewarding. I met many good friends and felt a great sense of accomplishment. As I began preparing for law school my senior year, I had to prepare the youth that I was involved with for my departure. However, I promised to stay in touch as best I could.

My senior year at Brown was a very busy time. I had many tasks to complete in what appeared to be a short time. The most immediate responsibilities included applying to law schools and doing an honors thesis while continuing my involvement in extracurricular activities and maintaining good grades.

I took the Law School Admission Test, the law school version of the SAT known as the LSAT. Unfortunately, like the SAT, I did not perform well on the LSAT. This was very frustrating since I had hoped, at the very least, that during my years at Brown my standardized test taking skills would improve. Perhaps it had, but there were no obvious signs of this when viewing my scores on the LSAT. My retake of the LSAT resulted in a lower score, which is even more rare. Thus, confronted with similar issues concerning my standardized test taking abilities, as when I applied to college, I was frustrated yet determined once again not to be deterred.

Like high school, I had maintained good grades at Brown and was even in the position of graduating cum laude. I had shown commitment to community and public service both by my involvement on and off campus. I had also made a strong connection with lawyers in the field and proved my worth both at New Haven Legal Assistance Association, where I worked during summers, and at Rhode Island Legal Services (RILS) during the school year. Robert Barge and Gary Powers of Rhode Island Legal Services also took me under their wing and prepared me for law school, even to the point of prepping me for the LSAT, law school interviews, and the material I would be presented. I could not let them or myself down.

I applied to several law schools of interest, including several Ivys, Howard University, and Northeastern University Law School. Gary Powers, one of my supervisors at RILS, had attended Northeastern University and recommended that I apply. Gary was a wonderful lawyer, who cared deeply about his clients. He was the type of lawyer I desired to become: smart, aggressive, and strongly committed to pursuing justice. Although my focus then was attending one of the Ivy League Schools, I applied to Northeastern after researching and learning about the commitment of its graduates to pursuing careers in public interest law, which was exactly the direction I was headed.

I asked several of my professors at Brown to write recommendations.

I was honest with them about my LSAT scores and expressed my strong desire to pursue a career in law. None of the professors I approached were reluctant in writing a recommendation for me and expressed strong support for my efforts. However, it was customary at Brown for the deans to write recommendations for each candidate seeking to enter graduate school. Moreover, students were given an assigned dean for this purpose.

When I informed my assigned dean of my intentions, he objected to me applying to law school and told me I probably would not get into any of the schools because of my LSAT score and it would hurt Brown's matriculation statistics. In turn, I pleaded with him to take notice of my success at Brown and put his personal feelings aside. To my surprise and dissatisfaction, he told me that he could not ignore my LSAT scores, and if I insisted in applying, I would have to do so without his recommendation.

This, I felt, was inconsiderate of him. I was not asking him to provide any false information. I was only asking him to highlight my qualities. I responded by trying to get a second dean to write for me, but she, too, refused. However, she agreed to speak with my assigned dean further. Weeks later, the dean called to tell me he would write the recommendation, but only if I applied to a new law school out west that was actively seeking to boost its minority enrollment. And very boldly, he handed me the pamphlet. I perused it carefully as I contemplated my response. I then politely declined and told him the school was not of interest to me and that I would apply to law school with or without his support.

After, I wondered how much my race and/or economic status factored into his stern and uncompromising position. I could not imagine him doing this to a White student. My psychology training took over, and I set out to learn his motivation. I shared this experience with a close friend who knew the dean well. He told me that it was a conscious decision on the Dean's part and probably little to do with race or my economic background. I was comforted to hear this from a friend I truly trusted and respected. However, the sting remained.

Still, I applied to law school. Within months, I received notice of my acceptance at Howard University with a full scholarship. I was delighted by Howard's confidence in me, especially since it is a school I had frequently visited with my youth organization and cherished. Moreover, I was in awe of the large number of Black leaders that graduated from Howard and the school's distinguished record in training civil rights leaders and lawyers.

Next, I was wait-listed at Columbia University School of Law. I was thrilled with the fact that Columbia was in New York City and possessed a fine reputation in placing students successfully upon graduation. The school also ranked high nationally. It was a school I could easily have attended.

Shortly after, I received an acceptance letter from Northeastern University School of Law. I had visited Northeastern previously and loved the commitment of the law school faculty and students; the varied curriculum; the public interest emphasis of the school; the smaller classes; the school's reputation as a premier public interest law school; its cooperative employment program, which emphasized and credited students for real life experience working in law firms; and other law-related institutions while in school. The only distraction from Northeastern for me was that it was in a city with a very volatile racial history: Boston, Massachusetts.

Within a month after receiving my law school admission letters, I declined Howard's offer of acceptance and wrote a letter telling the school how grateful I was to have been chosen. I accepted at Northeastern and waited out Columbia, though Columbia never changed its decision.

With my decision to attend Northeastern University School of Law settled, I refocused my attention on completing my honor's thesis at Brown. Brown required candidates for honors to write a thesis. In most disciplines, the student would write the thesis, have it approved by a single faculty member, and be awarded the honor diploma. However, at that time, students enrolled in independent study majors were required to have a committee of three faculty members, preselected by the student, approve the thesis. Since I was studying urban psychology, I selected two professors from Psychology and one from Sociology. Unknown to me at the time, my selection would haunt me later.

My committee of three consisted of Professor Lewis P. Lipsett and Professor Ferdinand Jones, both from the Psychology Department, and Associate Professor Phil Brown from Sociology. Professor Lipsett, a White male, was a wonderful professor and person and a nationally known expert in child psychology. I had previously taken courses with Professor Lipsett and enjoyed and respected his work. It also did not hurt that I usually received high grades in his class.

I also chose Professor Ferdinand Jones to chair the committee. I had known Professor Jones virtually since I entered Brown. He was a very insightful man, a clinical psychology specialist, and the head of Brown's Psychological Services Department, in addition to his teaching responsibilities. He was also the only Black professor in the Psychology Department. I had taken several courses with him and done well.

Last, I added Associate Professor Brown, a White male, who had only recently joined the Brown faculty in the sociology department as the third member of the team. I had taken one of his courses and enjoyed it. I particularly liked his approach in encouraging students to "think outside the box."

When selecting the committee, I had advised each professor of the topic of my thesis and asked if each was interested in serving as an advisor on the project. They agreed, and I went to work researching and writing my thesis on the entrapment of blacks in public housing. The thesis explored the history of public housing, the deplorable conditions residents of public housing were subjected to, and the racial identity and economic status of families relying on public housing because they were unable to afford alternative housing.

I spent nearly the entire year researching, writing, and rewriting my thesis, and keeping the advisers abreast of my progress. When I completed my thesis in March or April, I submitted it to the committee for comment and approval. While Professors Lipsett and Jones suggested minor changes, Professor Brown recommended that the thesis be changed to include economically disadvantaged Whites. This constituted a major change of focus as well as an unanticipated event. While his point was well received that poor Whites were also, in many ways, required to rely on public housing, there was no empirical research data to support his position that Whites were entrapped in public housing across the United States in 1981. I presented him with the relevant data and urged his support. He refused and told me he would only support me if I took the summer to amend the thesis to include Whites.

I objected to his position and took my grievance to a dean. I expressed my concern that while other disciplines were required to have one reader approve the thesis, it was unfair to require independent program concentrators to have approval of a unanimous committee of three. I suggested that the majority of two should be enough. The dean refused to override Professor Brown or to accept my argument regarding fairness. And since I refused to alter my position, I was unfairly denied conferment of the honor diploma.

This was a hard decision in view of what was at stake. I had worked so diligently to achieve high grades to obtain an honor degree. Receiving an honor diploma from Brown was extremely important to me. However, I did not have the guts to "doctor" my thesis to support what I knew to be an unsupportable position, that Whites were entrapped in public housing across the Unites States in 1981. This was true in the past, but it was not true in 1981. I was willing to kiss some butt, but I had my limit. I was not going to try to support the indefensible for the sake of pleasing the new professor on the block.

I therefore made a last ditch effort at suggesting that the thesis be read by another professor familiar with public housing, Elmer Cornwell, the chairperson of the Political Science Department, with whom I had done another housing project in the past, or a tenured and respected sociology professor, Dr. Martell. My suggestions were rejected out of hand. When I revisited the issue years later, I was told that another professor reviewed the thesis and agreed with the outcome. If true, this information was never communicated to me. Nor did this late revelation address the issue that independent study concentrators were unfairly being held to a higher standard than most undergraduates. If I had taken the easier route and stuck to one of the standard disciplines, I surely would have left Brown with my honor diploma in hand. Instead, I left with the memory of how close I came.

Reginald as a toddler.

Reginald's favorite pose in grammar school.

Reginald as a young attorney.

Reginald on a leisure walk in Nevada.

Reginald preparing to participate in his favorite recreational activity.

Reginald on vacation in Bermuda.

Reginald with wife, Charisse, on wedding day.

Reginald and Charisse before induction ceremony to
the New York State Supreme Court in 2017.

Induction ceremony, Hon Fern Fisher, Deputy Chief Administrative
Judge of the New York State Courts for NYC, preparing to
swear in Reginald to New York City Civil Court in 2009.

Reginald, Hon Fern Fisher (middle) and wife, Charisse Boddie (right).

My mother, Gladys Boddie, in the early years.

My mother at a holiday gathering in Florida. My niece is in
the center, and my sister Gwendolyn is on the right.

The last visit with my mother.

My brother Ronald at his college graduation in Atlanta, Georgia.
After years of working and raising a family, he decided to go to
college showing all things are possible with determination.

My sister Gwendolyn with one of my nieces.

Spending time in Hampton, Virginia, with aunt
Audrey on left and sister Sonia on right.

My favorite cruise photo with wife.

One of my most rewarding honors, receiving an NAACP Public
Service Award for my work on the bench and in the community.

Reginald and Charisse out for a summer evening event.

CHAPTER 6

Journey to Boston and Northeastern University School of Law

The summer of 1981 before entering law school, I returned to work as a legal assistant at New Haven Legal Assistance Association. On this occasion, I worked at the downtown office on Temple Street in the housing unit with attorneys Robert Solomon and John Alander, both graduates of Yale Law School. Both attorneys exhibited quiet demeanors yet were very astute, knowledgeable, and meticulous. They were excellent teachers and had high expectations for me. I was always happy to accept a challenge. As a result, we worked very well together and quickly became friends, as I had previously with their colleagues John Turner, Michael Sheehan, and Bruce Morrison, among others. This time I spent most of my nonwork hours trying to locate housing in Boston and obtain a student loan to pay for housing before the start of school in September. Both were traumatic experiences made less difficult by good friends.

Although Northeastern admitted and awarded me a full academic scholarship, it did not take much time to discover that apartments in Boston were quite expensive, and I would have to pay for it. As a result, it was necessary for me to obtain a loan and work to pay my living expenses. But even with careful planning and submission of my loan application in a timely manner, I was told my loan money would not be in hand until late October.

Consequently, I would not have the money to pay for housing and living expenses on the start date. When I shared this dilemma with Ms. Mininberg, to my pleasant surprise, she and her husband offered to use their contacts with New Haven Savings Bank to secure the money for me. They took out a personal loan for me with the agreement that I make the monthly payments of interest until my funds arrived and then pay the loan back. I am forever grateful that the Mininbergs were so committed to helping me realize my dream of becoming a lawyer that they risked their own assets. It was such a wonderful demonstration of support and love, and I remain forever grateful for them being in my life and intervening at this critical moment.

That summer, my good friend John Turner, then an attorney with New Haven Legal Assistance and now a supervising judge of the Superior Court in Connecticut, also stepped in to assist, without request. John previously attended law school in Boston. When he learned I would be attending Northeastern, he put me in touch with several of his friends in the area and gave me some pointers on locating housing. After securing the funds for housing, I arranged to go to Boston with my childhood friend, Robert Harriott Jr., with whom I had grown up on Ashmun Street. I searched the Boston newspaper in advance and made calls for appointments to see various apartments. On a Friday night, Robert and I took the bus from New Haven to Boston, with the intention of walking the streets early in the morning to see apartments. Saturday morning, we called to confirm the availability of each apartment. However, when we arrived at the various rental agencies less than a half hour later, we were repeatedly told the apartments were unavailable.

After tiring of this, when evening arrived, Robert and I decided to give up for the rest of the day. We did not have anywhere to stay since we had planned to secure an apartment and return home on a late bus. Instead, we decided to spend the night and try again the next day. We walked the streets until late and spent the night in a movie theater until it closed. At the time we were more interested in sleeping than we were in watching a movie. Consequently, we did not pay much attention to the title of the movie. As we were settling in to sleep, we heard laughs and hysterical moans. Only then did we realize we had mistakenly chosen an X-rated theater. Too tired to go into the streets, we rested until the theater closed. Around 4:00 a.m., we set back on the streets in a dangerous and unfamiliar neighborhood and walked until dawn. When daylight broke, we went to Boston University and spoke to students for leads, since that was the area I was most interested in living. Many sources recommended a realtor on Commonwealth Avenue.

When I called the realtor, I was told it had plenty of apartments. However, when Robert and I arrived twenty minutes later, we were told there were no vacancies.

I wondered how that could be possible. I then concluded that the realtors did not want to rent to me because of my color. I also realized for the first time that what some people had jokingly told me in the past really was true, I sounded like a White person on the telephone, but in person there was no denial that I was Black.

This experience was humiliating. They may well have just told me, "None of you are allowed here." It would have been just as clear and hurtful. And as much as I would have loved for these people to judge me by my character and not my color, there was no reasoning with them. As quickly as Robert and I arrived, we were escorted to the door as if we had dog feces on our shoes. My fears about Boston and the many stories I had read about the city's state of race relations became a reality, and at this point there was no backing out. Robert and I, feeling drained, decided to return home to recollect our thoughts and develop a new strategy. In the interim, I prayed for God to remove this barrier.

When I returned to work Monday morning, John Turner asked if my apartment search was successful. When I shared my experience with him, he offered to go to Boston with me. I felt a little guilty about a lawyer, who was so busy as head of the family law unit at legal services, taking time off to go with me all the way to Boston. However, I was elated and relieved that he had volunteered to do so. At the time, John was one of only a few Black attorneys who had ever worked for New Haven Legal Assistance. I had worked with him previously on several consumer cases as a law intern at the Dixwell

Neighborhood Office. He was quiet but extremely bright and very effective. I admired him because I was all too familiar with the struggles he likely faced as a Black man challenging injustice, based on the many books I had read and my own experiences. Therefore, I looked forward to spending personal time with him one-on-one.

We departed for Boston early in the morning and talked the entire trip. In the process, I learned a tremendous amount about how he grew up, why he came to New Haven, his law school experience, and his dreams. It was an invaluable experience and education for me. When we arrived in Boston, I saw John's quiet demeanor turn to constructive aggression. He asked me to show him the realty office that turned me down the prior week. We went directly there. I went to the exact same person. John asked if an apartment was available. This time the guy responded, "Yes, I have several." I nearly gasped for air. They volunteered information on the locations and offered to show me immediately. John then stepped out of the office as if to let off some steam or perhaps in a sigh of relief. While he was outside, the realtor asked me who he was. I was not going to ruin my chances of getting the apartment, so I simply replied, "A friend." The realtor showed us the apartment, which was entirely satisfactory, and had me sign the lease and make the deposit. The deal was sealed.

On the way home John revealed to me that the realtor probably thought he worked for the federal government as a housing discrimination tester. As I would later learn when reading Boston newspaper articles, he was right. The agency was being monitored for housing discrimination, and a lawsuit had already been filed and pending in court.

My neighborhood, in the Radcliffe Road area of Boston, was a very pleasant place to live. I enjoyed the neighborhood and the apartment building in which I lived immensely, and my neighbors were very kind and cordial. The selection of this apartment turned out to be an excellent decision, and I made it my home the entire time I lived in Boston.

Unlike other areas of Boston, there were few evident signs of racial tension in my neighborhood, although racial steering was obvious. The neighborhood, although devoid of a racial or ethnic mix, included an obvious mixture of incomes and family compositions ranging from low income to high income and single to families. Both Boston University and Boston College were also in proximity, which added to the cosmopolitan feel of the area and perhaps its more progressive leanings.

During my stay in Boston, I rarely felt the racial tensions in this neighborhood that I felt when visiting other areas, with just a couple of exceptions. The first was, of course, my initial rental experience. The second was when a group of White young men drove up to me several blocks from my apartment building, called me a nigger, and waited for my answer. I had been called similar ugly names before. But never had anyone called me such a name and waited for my answer to see what my next reaction would be. My initial thoughts for response were ugly. Instead, I kept walking, which led them to continue their rants, but it strengthened me. At that moment, I gained a better appreciation for how much strength it must have taken Dr. Martin Luther King Jr. and other civil rights protesters to restrain themselves when confronted with such vicious behavior. I truly wanted to retaliate but knew it was not in my interest to do so. Equally important, I felt that complaining to the Boston police was not an option, and even if I did, nothing would come of it.

Another racially charged incident occurred in the supermarket nearby, which I frequently visited and never personally had a problem. But on this day, the clerk was chastising a Hispanic couple about their alleged inability to speak English. Ironically, the couple was speaking English. The clerk told them essentially that they had been in America long enough to learn English. Witnessing this, I thought it was a mean and nasty thing to say to someone. I did not intervene. However, when the couple left the store, I walked out with them and explained my sorrow that the comment was made, because the truth is only Americans have the luxury of feeling they can rely on one language. People who come here from other countries usually speak several languages. Ironically, as I would also learn from speaking to the couple, they, like me, were graduate students in college.

Such foolhardy events abounded in Boston, although less so in my neighborhood.

For instance, there was an unwritten, yet enforced, code that Blacks entered South Boston at their own peril. South Boston was a haven for poor Whites and a focal point for violence against Blacks. This tension was fueled by the neighborhood's vicious response to forced busing to desegregate the schools, which required intervention by federal troops. A schism remained between Boston Blacks and Whites since.

Similarly, in Boston then, it was uncommon for Whites to safely visit parts of predominantly Black neighborhoods, like Roxbury and Dorchester, without placing themselves in harm's way. These areas often exhibited high crime and violence and were not well policed. As important, I quickly learned that there was a lot of animosity exhibited even within racial groups and ethnicities. Race relations overall in Boston were such as I had never witnessed anywhere before or ever again. Despite the less than ideal political and racial environment in Boston, I remained determined to succeed by making the best of the experience and to leave Boston as a newly minted lawyer.

My entering class at Northeastern University School of Law consisted of approximately 140 students and fifteen students of color, as we were referred to. The class derived from varied backgrounds. Most of the class members arrived straight from college, while others had advanced degrees and previous careers. Many students also had some interest in practicing public interest law in one form or another after law school. And since my career interests were the same, I immediately felt entirely comfortable at Northeastern. My Northeastern peers, wealthy and poor, seemed to be entirely in touch with their personal ambitions and the real world. Therefore, they would prove to be the welcome buffer I needed whenever I became frustrated living in Boston or pressured by the enormous amount of work required in law school. I looked forward to seeing them each day and having exciting conversations about mostly any topic.

The first year, I took a standard curriculum for law students: contracts, legal writing, criminal law, property, constitutional law, and evidence. The amount and intensity of work required me to make many adjustments in my life. Foremost, I had to adjust to carrying the large textbooks, which were quite heavy and rarely fit entirely in my briefcase. Adding to this difficulty, John Flym, the criminal law professor, had an unconventional habit of developing his own textbooks. Although quite interesting reading, the books consisted of several huge volumes of hundreds of pages on legal-sized paper. Carrying these books presented a physical challenge to my arms and back each day as I trekked with my weighty load from my apartment by subway to the Backbay neighborhood and then walked the remainder of the route to Northeastern.

The law school reading was voluminous and required in-depth analysis of each case, unless one took the risk of looking unprepared or unable to follow the class dialogue. This was a risk I usually did not take because I never felt comfortable being behind in assignments, but I know some students who did. So, I resorted to doing what seemed most appropriate to me even though it sometimes meant staying up studying half the night and attending classes early in the morning.

Unlike the anxiety-provoking stories frequently told about law schools that utilize the Socratic method of teaching, classroom participation at Northeastern Law School was more interesting and less intimidating because most professors did not call on students by surprise or seek to embarrass them into submission. Students at Northeastern were encouraged to volunteer, knowing if they did not, they could be called on at any time. This practice encouraged participation and students to ask questions or to state their disagreement with assertions made by others. It promoted better discussion. However, not all professors used this method.

Such was the case in my property law class taught by Professor Tom Campbell. Tom Campbell was trained at Harvard Law School, as were most Northeastern Law School professors. Northeastern had an unusual knack for hiring Harvard-trained professors, who all seemed to come to Northeastern en masse. Tom Campbell was, as one might imagine, a typical Harvard-looking professor, well dressed, often with a bow tie, wire rim glasses, and very formal, right down to the hand gestures and posture. He arrived each day and started timely, peppering students with questions about the case materials and insisting on appropriate legal answers, not based on opinion but law.

If Professor Campbell were to rephrase the often-repeated statement, "Tell me the truth and nothing but the truth," he would probably have said, "Tell me the law and nothing but the law." Students were permitted to share their opinions, but he made clear in his class, as any good lawyer knows, only the law counts. Consequently, although perhaps somewhat more conservative in his approach to teaching the law, as compared to many other Northeastern professors, he got his point across, and I like, other students, learned a great deal from him. I also grew to admire him.

In contrast, my criminal law professor had a very loose approach. Class discussion was almost strictly volunteer, and often the message was lost, not because of any lack of effort or communication on his part but because too often students used the class to share their personal opinions and to make political statements, ignoring the main legal concepts in the process. This sometimes left students, including myself, leaving the class feeling frustrated. Still, overall, I found the lecture format to be more comfortable.

The first year of law school required some major adjustments in my thinking. Most people are taught throughout their lives, either indirectly or directly, to be logical thinkers. Whereas previously, like most others, I learned to filter information through a logic prism, in law school we were taught to toss logic to the wind because the laws are not based on logic. Hence, we were forced to learn the law, often verbatim. Making such an adjustment requires a lot of training. Successful lawyers manage to do it. However, a lawyer's way of thinking is entirely different from the way most humans think. It is often said lawyers have a language and code of their own. I certainly found this to be true. Thus, law school might better be viewed as a method for retraining students in their thought processes while, in many cases, compelling them to discredit their previously learned mores and values.

As a result, my greatest challenge the first year was trying to learn as much as possible about the law, lawyers, and the way lawyers think while trying to preserve my values, mores, and integrity. This was no small challenge in view of the many pressures presented. The entire year I rarely had any free time, except late night on Saturdays when I usually tried to attend a party, the movies, or some other relaxing event. Otherwise, nearly every waking hour was dedicated to my legal studies.

When May arrived and my finals were completed, I was entirely exhausted. Still, I was so elated to have survived the process because not everyone did. Several of my classmates decided they could no longer handle the pressure or no longer desired to pursue a career in law after learning about the compromises that would be required in their lives, goals, and values. Such was the case with two of my close friends. The first had a bachelor and master's degree in psychology from Harvard. He was not only smart but a wonderful person to know and engage in conversation with. He left prior to the end of the year to pursue a career in counseling psychology. A second friend, whose father was a high-ranking official in Africa, left law school to join the family business by pursuing a career in politics at home. I yearned for their company, but I respected their choices.

When the first year ended, I looked forward to starting my summer law job. Northeastern, to my benefit, had a co-op program that allowed students upon conclusion of their first year of law school to alternate every three months between work and school. During these work semesters, students obtained jobs in law-related fields and received academic credit for successful completion. The Cooperative Education Program at Northeastern is unique in the sense that it allows students to gain real-life experience as part of the regular law school curriculum and obtain full academic credit. As a result, students learn the law by working in real-life situations handling cases and often are hired by the entities in which they work upon graduation from law school. This program not only reinforces the classroom content but does wonders for the resume. The Cooperative Education Program is one of the school's most popular attractions.

For my first co-op experience, the summer of 1982, I returned, for a third time, to New Haven Legal Assistance to work in the criminal law unit. This was an area of the law in which I had never previously worked and desired to learn more about. The criminal law unit consisted of Tom Corradino, managing attorney, Attorneys Stephen Frazzini and Elaine Gordon, and Lucille "Minnie" Anderson, paralegal.

Tommy Corradino, or "top cat" as I named him, because of his hearty laugh and the fact that he was the supervising attorney in the unit, was an extremely bright attorney and a wonderful guy to know. He worked extremely hard on cases and was very well-known and respected in the community. Although he was my primary supervisor, we did not spend a great deal of time together because of his very busy schedule. He simply gave me assignments and expected the work to be completed in a timely manner.

In contrast, Minnie and I spent a lot of time together since she was the only staff paralegal and investigator in the unit. Minnie and I found ourselves often discussing the details of criminal investigations she was assigned. The case that has always stood out in my mind was a rape case in which the alleged victim stated she was sexually attacked in her bedroom and able to identify the assailant by his hands. She was otherwise unable to identify the assailant by height, weight, or any other characteristics.

I am very sympathetic to women who have been sexually assaulted in any way.

I have known many women who have suffered similar attacks, and it is a horrific crime. However, it did not seem plausible to me that the crime could be solved by identifying the assailant by his hands, absent any other distinguishable characteristics. Minnie agreed. At the direction of Mr. Frazzini, she and I set out to survey the neighborhood taking pictures of young Black men's hands to help prove the difficulty of identifying a Black man by his hands.

We visited the Dixwell area since this was the area we both lived previously and could expect to find the most cooperative people. After assuring the subjects that we were not working for the police and they were not in any sort of trouble, we took many pictures of Black men's hands. We delivered the pictures to Mr. Frazzini. Just when I had hoped my work on the case was completed, Mr. Frazzini asked if I would don a Black ski mask, as had the alleged assailant, and appear in court at the trial to see if the victim could identify me. Although perhaps this might have been an exciting experiment for other law students, I was unable to get past the idea of putting myself in the humiliating position of donning a ski mask to see if a woman would falsely accuse me of committing a crime.

The scenario raised too many connotations for me to stomach, so I politely refused the request. My first response was not quickly accepted, prompting Mr. Frazzini to inquire further as to my reasons. I simply told him the scenario provoked too much anxiety in me. That actually was the truth, put diplomatically. The real facts are I had spent my entire life trying to stay clear of any criminal record, and placing myself in such a position to be falsely accused, even if only as an experiment, provoked too much anxiety in me. Mr. Frazzini ultimately respected my decision, even if he may not have completely understood it at that time, and I was grateful never to have to deal with the issue again. As might be expected, I did not attend the trial.

Another very memorable moment that summer occurred when I appeared in court with Elaine Gordon. Ms. Gordon had assigned me to assist in handling several juvenile delinquency cases. It was customary for lawyers representing defendants to arrive at the courthouse early to have a conference with the prosecutor to see if a lower charge, lesser penalty, or dismissal could be obtained. On this day, Ms. Gordon gave me specific instructions regarding a strategy on several cases, told me to go to court to make the request, and she would meet there later.

I arrived at court early and well-dressed. There were two lines of people waiting to speak with the prosecutor, one for attorneys and another for defendants. I stood in the line for attorneys. The prosecutor, a White male, without asking who I worked for, simply assumed I was a defendant because of my color and told me I was in the wrong line. After I explained who I worked for, he recoiled, realizing he had just outed himself in front of everyone, and nothing he said could explain the impression he had created. He did not even offer an apology. Instead, he proceeded forward and just asked what case I wanted to discuss.

The assumption that I was a criminal accused of a crime simply because of my skin color hurt deeply, but I tried in earnest to hide it. I had grown somewhat accustomed to blatant racism in Boston, but here it was, right in the backyard where I grew up. It was hard to overlook the fact that there remained a long way to go in this area. As hard as I tried to overlook this event, when Ms. Gordon arrived a half hour later, a second incident occurred.

Elaine Gordon, who is White, had arranged to have a conference about one of our cases in a side room. When she and the other attorneys proceeded to enter a side room to discuss the case, I followed. This time another White attorney stated to her, "your client must wait outside." She immediately retorted, "This is not my client. He works for my office." She quickly embarrassed the attorney about making assumptions about race, and to this day I have always admired her for the way she handled the situation. Her approach both made clear that she will not tolerate such assumptions being made about her workers or Black people and left the attorney with something to think about the next time he would encounter a similar situation.

As I later learned, I would frequently be mistaken for a client many more times than I would like to admit by attorneys and judges. But I left New Haven Legal Assistance that summer at the end of my internship with many successful outcomes for the clients as well as great admiration for Ms. Gordon. I truly appreciated her no-nonsense style and made it my business to work on as many cases as possible with her. She was also the first attorney to introduce me to the art of schmoozing to get the desired results. She was a classy act.

When the summer ended, I was excited about being a second-year law student. My return to campus in September went smoothly. My friends and I were all very excited about seeing each other and sharing our summer work experiences. We were equally excited about surviving the first year of law school, which is the most difficult, and progressing to take courses of personal interest.

I took several courses of personal interest my second year. However, the course I remember best was civil rights litigation with Professor Denise Carty-Bennia. Professor Carty-Bennia was a very strong-minded Black woman. She usually was either very nice or very intimidating, depending on the person or subject involved. She was remarkably bright and extremely knowledgeable about the law, especially on issues of concern to Black people, legal and otherwise. You either liked her or you did not. At times, I personally swayed to both sides.

Nevertheless, I held her in esteem because she was the only professor of African American ancestry on the entire law school faculty then. As a result, she alone carried the burden of presenting and defending issues of concern to students of color at the law school on the faculty level. Moreover, she was usually outspoken and very effective.

My good friend Elizabeth Yampierre, now executive director of a New York City organization, first introduced me to Denise, with a warning about watching my toes if I ever challenged her. And I could tell from personal intuition that Denise was a very intense and complex person.

Denise taught the second half of my evidence class during my first year of law school, which allowed me to get to know her better. She was, as I assumed, very intense but always well prepared and informative. She peppered her lessons not only with textbook information but her personal experiences as a practitioner and masterful tricks of the trade which she found effective. This added excitement to her lessons, especially in contrast to some of the other teachers I had. Familiar with her dynamic style, I looked forward to hearing what she had to say about civil rights issues, an area of the law of special interest to me since at the time I had planned to pursue a career as a civil rights lawyer. Denise did not disappoint the class. She added colorful history and explanations to her discussion of the laws, many times interpreting them in ways most lawyers might never consider, not for lack of intellect but because creativity is not always condoned in interpreting laws. She expressed the importance of creativity and focusing on detail.

I still remember the shock both I and my classmates experienced when we learned that the Emancipation Proclamation did not free all the slaves but simply permitted free slaves to remain free, contrary to what we had been taught in our previous history classes. We also learned that Rosa Parks was already seated in the back of the bus when she was asked to give up her seat. Thus, she really was not in violation of the law. The driver just had the audacity to ask her to move further back.

Another enlightening example was when I learned that after University of Texas Law School refused to integrate, the school was sued. This resulted in the decision in *Sweatt v. Painter*, which led to the mandate by the US Supreme Court that the state provide an equal law education for Black students. In a further effort to avoid integrating the University of Texas Law School, the State created Texas Southern Law School for Black students, which ironically was the school my older brother David, a now retired judge in Washington, DC, attended.

The education I received from Professor Carty-Bennia was invaluable. She also provided me an opportunity to share my personal experiences with the class of my mother in the *Boddie v. Connecticut* case. I shared that the case reaffirmed divorce as a fundamental right guaranteed by the US Constitution and helped set in motion court fee waivers for indigent persons and was one of the first of many class actions won in the US Supreme Court by legal services. However, despite the success of the case, which challenged the payment of fees for divorce of indigent persons, my mother was forced to pay because by the time the case was decided, she had acquired full-time employment as a nurse's assistant. I also shared that due to the lengthy litigation process, the case also delayed my mother's divorce for many years.

And for all this, my mother indicated she never fully understood the significance of the case until my brother David began law school and reported that the case was being taught in law schools around the country. I therefore implored my classmates to ensure clients understand the significance of their cases so they become matters of pride for the client as well as the lawyer. Despite my mother's well-documented victory with the high court, I also shared that locally my mother was better known for her activism and involvement in legal challenges against the New Haven Housing Authority, seeking quality repairs and fair transfer policies.

As the year continued, Professor Carty-Bennia grew to know me better as a person, instead of the elite snobbish minority she apparently thought I was. As a result, we grew closer and began to share more personal life experiences with each other. Out of this relationship, I grew to admire her, and she acquired greater respect for me. Our mutual respect continued to grow when I became the class representative on the school-wide admissions committee.

Northeastern Law School had two admissions committees, a minority committee headed by Professor Carty-Bennia and a school-wide committee. Minority students could gain admission through either route. However, all other students were admitted by the school-wide committee. Students were included on both committees. However, class members were elected to serve as representatives on the school-wide admissions committee. These representatives had a vote equal to all other members of the school committee, including the director of admission and faculty. The school-wide committee could also veto any vote of the minority admissions committee, although this was a rare event.

During the fall of 1983, after some brief campaigning and interviewing, I was elected to serve as the class representative on the school-wide admissions committee. This was both a wonderful honor and a tremendous responsibility. Each representative was required to read approximately twenty to thirty files weekly, along with a designated partner, and make a presentation and recommendation at the weekly admissions committee meeting. This required a tremendous amount of reading in addition to my regular work, as well as a lot of contemplation.

Northeastern University Law School received applications from all over the country. Most of the applicants held leadership posts in college and beyond and had already began careers as paralegals, teachers, or in other fields. Most of the applicants exhibited great accomplishments. Therefore, the real focus became which students truly deserved to be admitted to Northeastern University School of Law. This was an enormously challenging task as we looked closely at courses taken, grades, difficulty of the courses selected, class rank, LSAT scores, personal statements, personal achievements, extracurricular activities, and recommendations.

To my surprise, the members of the committee often agreed on most candidates who were either admitted or denied admission. However, a third group of candidates fell in the gray area, and these matters were usually resolved amicably through an internal process that I cannot disclose. At other times, some wrangling took place which either led to success by the faculty or the students. Regardless, at the end of the admissions season, we all left feeling better for having participated in helping contribute to the school's future and learning more about each other in the process.

While serving on the committee, I also had an opportunity to return to Brown as a recruiter for the law school and having the same deans who refused to write a recommendation for me request a private audience to pitch their favorite candidates. Having nearly fallen victim to these tactics when I was applying to law school while a student at Brown, I insisted upon meeting all the interested students and speaking with them directly. This served to maximize the number of applicants to Northeastern as well as help me become personally familiar with the students.

Weeks after my recruitment visit to Brown, I learned the deans were not comfortable with my approach and sought Northeastern schedule a second visit to the school. I made sure that did not take place. We had already visited the school and achieved our goal. We got the applicant pool we desired. It was of no interest to me or Northeastern that any dean preferred an opportunity to pitch his/her favorite candidates. We simply had no time for such nonsense. And of my group, at least one student was admitted, who is now a very successful attorney in New Jersey.

By the end of the academic quarter, I had grown to be quite comfortable at Northeastern. Not only had I developed a workable study schedule that permitted me sufficient time to sleep, I had found some pleasure in supplementing my schedule, tutoring undergraduate students at Northeastern in math and English, working as a swimming instructor at the local YMCA on Huntington Avenue, and continuing my service on the admissions committee.

During my tenure at the YMCA, I made many friends in the community and organized the first Black youth swimming team in the state. Although I describe the team as Black, this was more about how it was perceived than in actuality. The team consisted mostly of Black swimmers but was the only fully integrated youth swimming team in the state. This made for an interesting dynamic because most places we visited were not accustomed to seeing inner-city youth of color compete as swimmers, not to mention a fully integrated team. Truthfully, I had taught swimming many years prior in different capacities and had never witnessed such either. However, the Boston YMCA was receptive to the idea, and I was willing to give it my best effort. So, we practiced during the week, and on Saturdays, I looked forward to taking the youth, ages eight to fourteen, to different cities and towns throughout Massachusetts to compete. Initially we finished in last place. As time passed, team members won first through third place in their individual and group events, and the other teams began to take notice. Although the team never won a team championship, we won considerable respect for our progress in holding our own in the league. Our efforts and progress also helped enhance the children's self-esteem.

In December 1982, I began a new academic quarter in cooperative employment. I stayed in Boston so I could remain in my apartment and monitor the progress of my swimming team at the YMCA while I worked at the Lawyers' Committee for Civil Rights Under Law of the Boston Bar Association, a civil rights law center affiliated with the Boston Bar Association. Upon my arrival at the Lawyers' Committee for Civil Rights, I was a little surprised to see there were no attorneys of color on the staff. Although I certainly did not have any issues with Whites working in a civil rights organization, I expected a more racially diverse staff. But this was not the case in Boston. There was, however, one attorney who boasted he was a representative since he spoke Spanish, although he was not of Hispanic descent. This argument probably would not be given much credence any other place, but this was Boston.

Despite these obvious inconsistencies, I had a wonderful time working at the Lawyers' Committee as a legal intern, which was ably directed by Judy Tracey, a remarkably bright attorney and unusually nice person. She sought to engage me in every aspect of litigation, including observation of trials, as well as encourage my participation in strategy and administrative meetings at the bar association. As a result, I learned a great deal about the strategic planning of civil rights cases and the need to solicit professional and public support for the cases and amass finances to sustain the litigation.

I also remember well my work with Robert Sherman, who headed the racial violence project at the office. His work often took him into neighborhoods to promote efforts to quell racial violence, educate the public about the damages of racial violence to race relations, and seek prosecution of people charged with engaging in unlawful acts of racial violence. Robert made frequent trips to South Boston, where a high incidence of racially motivated violence occurred against Blacks. The violence in the area was so well-known that it was common knowledge that any Black who entered the area entered at risk of loss of "life and limb."

Robert and I often discussed his work. From time to time he would bounce ideas off me as well. I did not mind sharing my opinions. However, eventually he asked that I visit South Boston with him. I agreed. After reflection, I became terrified. Like most others, I had read the many newspaper articles about racial violence in South Boston. Also lurking in my mind was my own experience when I made a wrong turn off the highway with my youth group from Providence years prior. Not knowing we were in South Boston, a group of South Boston residents trapped the kids in a fast-food restaurant when they entered to use the restroom while I waited outside thinking they were horsing around. When they returned to the van twenty minutes later, they shared their experience. I was shocked beyond belief. Still not certain they had told the truth, I asked a gentleman at a gas station nearby for directions. He told me where I was and cautioned me not to ask anyone else in the area any questions if I wanted to make it home alive.

At that time, I also had a cousin who resided on the border of South Boston and insisted I never visit the neighborhood alone out of fear of what could happen to me. She shared stories of violent encounters with many of her neighbors as well as unsuspecting visitors to the area. Consequently, I did not have any real urge to go to South Boston, even walking alongside Robert.

Robert perceived that I was afraid when he told me the date we would visit and shared with me that he had sent the word out in advance that I was not to be harmed. This comforted me tremendously, although I did not tell him so at the time. I really trusted Robert, and he always did as promised. And so, I went to South Boston trying to ignore everything I had heard and read about the neighborhood. To my delight, I had a wonderful visit to the neighborhood and courthouse. I was grateful to have visited and survived the trip, but I never went back.

When the winter co-op ended, it was back to school. I was much better for having had the experience of working at the Lawyers' Committee for Civil Rights Under Law. I returned to school understanding a great deal more about the city of Boston, its legal community, and its politics. It was a tremendous learning experience. At school, I diligently worked through my courses, as in the past, looking forward to going off again to work for the summer. And I would not be disappointed.

The summer of 1983, I obtained an internship at Neighborhood Legal Services, in Hartford, Connecticut, where I handled employment discrimination cases. Although I grew up in Connecticut, I had never spent much time in Hartford. As a result, I thought working at Neighborhood Legal Services would provide me an opportunity to learn more about Connecticut's capital city and enhance my employment law knowledge.

Neighborhood Legal Services had a comprehensive employment law unit that handled employment discrimination cases from the administrative complaint process through trial. Consequently, it provided me the opportunity to gain experience handling employment discrimination cases from start to finish under the student practice rules. The complaints were filed with the EEOC, located just next door, and proceeded in court if they were not resolved administratively. I drafted complaints and participated in settlement of cases. I also assisted with case preparation for trials and attended both federal and state hearings. The only drawback to the entire summer was that

I had to get up very early in the morning to meet my carpool for the ride to Hartford from New Haven every day. The commute was exhausting and left me with little energy to socialize in the evening with friends upon return home. However, the interaction during the ride was invaluable since I was the youngest rider among a group of mostly insurance company executives, who discussed the intimate details of their workday.

I did manage to eke out several weekends where my friends and I returned to Hartford during evenings to socialize and learn more about the city. Although these moments were few, they were a lot of fun. At the conclusion of the summer, it was back to Boston again. However, this time when I returned to Boston, things were very different. I found myself immensely focused on just completing my third year of studies so that I could get on with my life and leave Boston. I never grew to like Boston, although I met many people in Boston I truly came to admire. Still, I just wanted to leave as soon as possible.

My last year in law school I took exciting courses that I had a great interest in, including corporations, tax, and conflicts of law. The content was interesting, as were the teachers. I also found it exciting that the teachers permitted students with differing views to voice their opinions. The comments of sound substance worked to the benefit of the entire class and often helped elucidate otherwise tedious legal concepts. However, not unlike some other classes I have participated in, there was also a group of students who appeared to talk for the purpose of hearing themselves talk. This provided good entertainment as the class grew to know who these people were. Such was the dynamics of the law school classroom, always interesting, especially if you enjoy interpreting social interaction.

In December 1983, I was selected for what was then one of the most popular and sought-after cooperative employment experiences at Northeastern—working at the Center for Constitutional Rights in New York City. It was no small matter that CCR was a nationally recognized civil rights institution that had successfully litigated major civil rights cases on prominent constitutional issues. Many would say it was a leading force in litigation involving constitutional issues. CCR's staff and board included several widely known and recognized attorneys, including Arthur Kinoy, Randolph Scott-McLaughlin (now Randolph McLaughlin), William Kunstler, and Betty Lawrence Bailey, among others.

As I embarked on my daily commute to CCR from New Haven, I received only a small stipend from the school that covered my travel and basic expenses. Nevertheless, I always believed you must go to an opportunity. Therefore, I did not have any problem getting up every morning at 6:00 a.m. to commute from New Haven to New York City by train. To save some money, I often walked from Grand Central train station to the office on Fourteenth Street or the return route. Each day, I arrived on time, excited to be there and full of energy.

Initially, I worked with Betty Lawrence Bailey. She educated me on some novel approaches in using federal laws to bring wrongdoers to justice. One such case involved a civil suit against the Ku Klux Klan. For all its cases, the center regularly held strategy meetings with staff, board members, and attorneys around the country in pursuit of positive outcomes. Every resource available was pursued, and CCR's record of success was astounding. You had to take notice, and I did. I tried to learn everything I could.

Weeks into my internship, I began working with Randolph McLaughlin. He first assigned me multiple reading tasks to insure I knew the necessary statutes and laws applicable to the cases. Next, he assigned me a difficult and challenging task as if to test my work ethic. I quickly completed the task and asked for more. He shared that he was impressed and began involving me in his meetings both in and outside the office, which allowed me to meet and become friends with Arthur Kinoy and William Kunstler, both whom I knew to be legal legends. I always tried to stay calm in their presence. I spoke to them both as if I had always known them, and they responded in kind.

I grew close to Randy, and we worked closely on several cases. The case I remember best involved the State's efforts in shutting down a minority-owned nursing home for alleged violations. I researched the health laws and guidelines, and Randy and I created a strategy for the hearing, which was scheduled to be held in Albany. He and I reviewed thousands of documents contained in numerous big boxes. This was the first time I had examined such a voluminous number of documents. However, Randy aided my task by teaching me how to glance many pages at a time looking for certain clues or patterns and tagging items of concern.

Weeks later, we carted the boxes in his car for the trip to Albany, where we remained for several days. As we departed New York City, it began to snow. By the time we arrived upstate, we were in the middle of a massive snowstorm. But we were determined. We continued our journey, and the hearing proceeded, as scheduled.

When we stepped into the administrative hearing room, the attorneys on the other side were totally unprepared for us. They evidently thought the hearing would be a quick event. When they saw multiple boxes of thousands of documents, they displayed a look of surprise on their faces. We were able to pull evidence from the boxes with ease. As they sought to make out each allegation of their case against our client, we picked a document from our boxes for use with ease in defending the client. By the end of the hearing, we were all exhausted. Though we did not prevail in the end, our client was grateful for our efforts in defending the nursing home.

In the process, Randy and I grew to know a considerable amount about each other. I also met and learned a considerable amount about his family and upbringing. We discussed successes and failures and the different paths our lives had taken. We learned that we had a great deal in common. As a result, I not only learned an immeasurable amount of law but concluded the internship feeling I had acquired a new extended family.

When I returned to school, I intensified my efforts to locate employment as a civil rights lawyer. I was most interested in working at the Center for Constitutional Rights. However, CCR did not have any vacancies for a staff attorney. Moreover, decently paid civil rights work was not easy to locate. As a result, I applied for jobs in the US Justice Department, Civil Rights Division, in Washington, DC, Legal Aid Society in New York City, and legal services in Philadelphia, Pennsylvania. I was wait-listed for the honor's program at the Justice

Department but had the department accepted me, I probably would have taken advantage of the opportunity because I was thrilled with the idea of being in the center of Washington politics. Instead, I refused a generous offer to work in the employment law unit of legal services in Philadelphia to work at the Legal Aid Society in New York City.

I found the Legal Aid Society attractive because the organization serviced the largest number of indigent people in New York City, had wonderful people, and offered me a modest salary, though less than I had been offered to go to Philadelphia. I also anticipated coming to New York would open a wide range of opportunities for a prosperous legal career. Moreover, Paul Klein, the director of recruitment at the Legal Aid Society, made sure he did everything to ensure that the organization did not overlook me as a candidate. Thus, in late April, just when I started leaning toward Philadelphia because of its employment discrimination unit, the Legal Aid Society made an offer which I accepted.

With my future employment established, I looked forward to completing law school with the best grades possible. I did extremely well. And to my surprise, my class also selected me to be the graduation speaker. I was deeply honored by the selection as well as their approval of the community work I had done at Northeastern. However, the honor proved to be short-lived. Ironically, the newly appointed dean of the law school and my previous torts professor, whom I perceived to be a kind, caring, and sensitive person, notified me that if I were to speak, he needed to critique my speech.

Although I knew he was within his rights of asking me to adhere to certain school standards, I was insulted that he felt a need to critique every word of my graduation speech. I therefore assured him that I would not do anything to embarrass or otherwise diminish the reputation of the school, hoping this would put the issue to rest. It did not. Consequently, I relinquished the opportunity to give the speech rather than give in to his request.

This, in many ways, reminded me of the experience I had at Brown University surrounding my honors thesis. Again, someone I fully trusted placed me in an awkward position, wanting to manipulate me. And once again, the loss of a wonderful opportunity would be at my expense. I wondered, as difficult as it was, if I should concede or stand on my principles and walk out with my head high.

I chose to maintain my respect and dignity and continue to be an example. I felt compelled to do more than simply give lip service when it came to defense of my integrity, but it really hurt. As the graduation speech was delivered in May 1984 by a fellow classmate, I could only imagine what could have been if I had relented. According to the best information available at the time, I would have been the first Black student elected to give the law graduation speech, and what a speech it would have been. I had planned to mention all the great things about Northeastern Law School, the cooperative employment program, the committed professors, the wonderful alumni always willing to step in to help in any way possible, the great future of the school, the wonderful spirit of cooperation among the students, and how I benefited from attending Northeastern. Yes, I had everything to gain by discussing the greatness of Northeastern Law School, and I was not going to disparage the school or myself in the process.

Looking back, I saw a great moment lost for myself and the school.

CHAPTER 7

Life after Law School

After receiving my Juris Doctor degree from Northeastern University School of Law, I remained in Boston for the summer to study for the bar examination. Each morning, I attended bar preparation classes and spent the remainder of the day studying at the Boston University School of Law library. It would seem that law students would know everything they need to know to take the bar examination after attending and successfully completing law school. However, the specialized bar preparation courses, much like the LSAT and SAT, showed me how much more we really needed to know, or should I say memorize to the point of exhaustion. The heat and unfriendly environment in Boston did not make my circumstances any easier. After all, most of my law school friends had departed the city. I remained in Boston because it was one of the few cities outside New York State conducting the preparation course for the New York Bar Examination. Consequently, it made sense for me to remain in my apartment for a couple more months before moving. I tolerated Boston for the time and was extremely elated to leave when the summer ended.

Upon arrival in New York City, my first assignment at Legal Aid was as an attorney in the social security unit of the Brooklyn office, which ironically was located in Manhattan at 11 Park Place. The unit was a new project overseen by a supervisor whom I later learned preferred hiring women. Despite the less than welcoming circumstances, I tried to make the best of the situation. I worked hard to learn as much as I could about social security, both for retired persons and those with disabilities, although my unit handled mostly disability claims. In the course of my time with the social security unit, I handled hundreds of claims for people seeking disability for all types of medical reasons, including psychiatric. Although most claims were resolved with successful advocacy through contact with the social security administration, others required a hearing and, in some cases, an appeal following an adverse hearing decision.

Handling such claims required very meticulous work, including contact with physicians for reports, ability to decipher the medical language in the reports, as well as doctors' handwriting, and knowing how to fit the cases squarely within the social security regulations. Both my knowledge of the law and ability to be firm in my position about the clients' qualifications for social security were frequently tested by some judges whenever I attended a social security hearing. But I was rarely rattled, even by the sometimes off-put behavior displayed by one or more of them in slamming items on the table or yelling at my clients for effect. And when it bothered me, I refused to give them the satisfaction of knowing it. Eventually, I gained the respect of most of the judges and their cooperation in not trying to dismantle my clients' cases before hearing all the facts.

After handling hundreds of social security disability cases, regularly hearing and having contact with people who have serious psychiatric and other medical problems, I eventually found myself wondering about there being so many sick people in the world. The stories were heart-wrenching and, many times, simply depressing. Truly, I was sensitive to my clients' problems and felt their pain, but I needed to supplement these depressing stories with more positive circumstances.

To assist me in this process, I asked attorneys in the general litigation unit at the office if I could accompany them to court on some of their cases. The director of the office Morton Dicker, who would also eventually become a good friend and mentor, allowed me to go to court with the attorneys and handle a variety of the cases. As a result, I was able to learn a tremendous amount about handling housing cases as well as other general civil matters, from the beginning through trial. Janise Robinson and Daniel Ashworth were of special assistance in this regard. Both became my personal mentors. I tried to learn everything I could from them. I also participated in as many training events as was possible. I was determined to make a mark. In the process, I achieved a great amount of success with my cases. After I developed a special interest and focus in handling housing matters, I left Legal Aid to work in a specialized housing unit at Harlem Legal Services.

At the time, Harlem Legal Services was rebuilding its housing unit under the direction of Fern Fisher. I felt I could make a significant contribution. I interviewed with the office and loved the energy of the attorneys in the unit. When the offer of employment was made the day after my interview, I was overjoyed and accepted immediately.

My work at Harlem Legal Services provided considerable opportunities to enhance my litigation and trial skills in a comfortable and supportive environment. The dedication of Fern to the unit's development and quality work was a major factor in the unit's success. The unit consisted of a close group of attorneys, including Fern, Ignatius Chibututu, Khalick Hewitt, Michael Parris, Phillip Krug, and myself. We met regularly to discuss case strategies and assisted each other in our work. Although we each had our personal approaches to cases, we had a consistent and unified goal, providing the best legal services for indigent people in Harlem. To this end, we did not waver, and we left no stone unturned. We were very effective in preventing evictions in most of the cases we handled. I felt tremendous satisfaction being affiliated with such a wonderful team of attorneys who, in addition to being my colleagues, became good friends.

When Fern took maternity leave, I was tapped to oversee the unit during her temporary absence. As I look back today, it was this early opportunity and experience that enhanced my confidence and abilities in supervising attorneys. The experience also added a great deal of responsibility. While missing Fern, I proceeded with fervor in carrying out unit meetings and monitoring the caseloads and progress of my colleagues as well as handling my own share of cases. The attorneys, in turn, were incredibly cooperative, and we made tremendous progress in our work, consequently also cementing our relationship. The relationship among this group of attorneys has withstood time and remains strong even today.

When Fern returned from maternity leave, I felt prepared to expand my responsibilities at Harlem Legal Services. I requested and began handling cases outside the unit as well. I was still enjoying my work at Harlem Legal Services immensely when I learned of a civil rights opportunity at the Center for Law and Social Justice from another close friend, Wendy Brown.

I had met Wendy many years earlier doing committee work with the National Conference of Black Lawyers. I respected and admired her a great deal as an attorney. When I learned of the opportunity to work alongside her at the Center for Law and Social Justice at Medgar Evers College, located in Brooklyn, New York, it was an opportunity I could not refuse.

I applied for the position at the civil rights research, litigation, and public policy advocacy organization, around September 1988. I had a very intense interview with Esmeralda Simmons, Esq., the executive director and a very prominent Black leader in New York City and State. In November, I was hired.

I was elated to work in a civil rights organization and truly felt I had arrived. Initially, I did research and other work on a major voting rights case concerning broken voter machines during the first Jesse Jackson campaign for president and served as the lead person on a trade school fraud case and a related bankruptcy matter. I was totally in my element, surrounded by attorneys, researchers, policy analysts, and political activists. But soon after, I was saddened to learn that Wendy would be moving on to teach at a law school in New Orleans.

The announcement caught me totally off guard. Still, I was happy for her. Months later, an executive director position at Harlem Legal Services became available, and I was invited to apply. It was a position I had a lot of interest in. But I chose not to apply since I did not want to leave the center after having only recently arrived. In hindsight, I probably should have applied because it was a great opportunity, and the chance to gain the position at that office never presented itself again. And no matter how much you like your colleagues, there is nothing like being the boss.

After Wendy left the center, I gained more responsibility, including a regular litigation docket, and supervision of one or more members of the police and racial violence and public relations project. My supervisory work, as might be expected, included a review of other employees' work, review of monthly reports, drafting reports, litigation, grant writing, media appearances, and other tasks. Eventually I supervised the entire police and racial violence project and helped create and apply for funding for a law education project in the New York City Public Schools, in which lawyers from the center visited selected schools in Community School District 16 to teach law to middle school students and evaluate their progress.

As the center usually handled class action lawsuits involving hundreds, if not thousands of plaintiffs, the legal work was very complex and intense yet rewarding. These responsibilities presented wonderful learning experiences and growth for me. This made for a very busy schedule on my part and little leisure time.

Around this time, my long-term girlfriend and I parted company. She was a wonderful person. However, as people often do, we grew apart. The termination of this relationship left a void. The search for my next girlfriend was fruitless until I returned to visit friends at Harlem Legal Services two years later.

On that visit, I saw a young lady with whom I had worked previously. After I said hello, she reminded me that I once agreed to take her out to lunch. I promised this time I would and called the same week. We went on a dinner date, which was all I had intended at the time. However, we began seeing each other regularly after, and in April 1990 we married.

Things went smoothly for the first year, with minor issues here and there, but nothing out of the ordinary for new couples living together trying to accommodate the normal personality variations and differences of personal preference. To a great extent, the progress of the first year even exceeded my expectations. She was advancing on her job, and we purchased and moved into a new home. By all assessments we were on the fast track.

Shortly after we moved, I adopted her child. The child did not have a relationship with her biological father, and having grown up without a father in my life, I did not want her to have the same experience. I loved her as if she were my own child, and if you saw us together, you would not have presumed otherwise. Therefore, I was prepared and committed to formalizing the relationship by fulfilling such an obligation and important role for her for a lifetime. Her mother agreed and commenced the case, and the adoption took place.

However, as my relationship with my daughter grew incrementally, the relationship between myself and her mother grew apart. And before I could fully comprehend how we had arrived at a seemingly endless point of contention toward each other, the mother was spending all her time at work, school, or church. I was eventually confronted with the unbearable truth, that the marriage would never work. It was extremely difficult for me to walk through the doors of a church after that, although I did.

I maintained my faith in God and to be led, as in the past, to make the right life decisions. I prayed mightily about whether to divorce. I knew well the effects of divorce, having been raised in a single-parent household. This is not to say that single parents cannot do an excellent job raising children. However, there can be little question that single-parent households often present more challenges in raising children than two-parent households. However, in the end, I was left with little choice.

After expensive litigation, coupled with the mother's stated intention never to cooperate amicably, we agreed to terminate the adoption. In doing so, I had hoped the mother would see the benefits of still having me involved in the child's life. However, this expectation never materialized.

After, I spent many days and nights wondering what would come of my bright little girl who loved learning, meeting new friends, and once bragged to her entire class about me being able to braid her hair and that "my dad can fix anything." She was so clever she could even get me to laugh at my expense. Such was the case when I took her to the grocery store, and she wanted some mints. I knew she liked the mints, but that day I was determined not to buy any and hoped she would not ask. When we got to the cashier, in the presence of a full line of people, she asked for the mints. When I responded, "Not today," she said, "But, Daddy, don't you need them for your breath?" Everyone laughed. Surely, I was not going to embarrass myself by saying no with a full line of people laughing at me. I was so astonished by her cleverness that I proudly purchased the mints.

Many times, I wondered whether my bright child, with everything going for her, might have it all destroyed due to circumstances entirely beyond her control. It reminded me of the circumstances of all too many children I had observed in my many different capacities working with children. I had always attempted to intervene on the children's behalf to improve their situation in any way I could, yet I felt entirely helpless when it came to protecting my own daughter. Her mom was not thinking rationally, and there was nothing I could do about it. Eventually, I lost all contact with my daughter, though we would reunite years later.

As these events unfolded, I tried my best to remain focused on my work at the Center for Law and Social Justice. It was not easy, but I managed with the support of my colleagues. I found myself intensely focused on work, perhaps to the point of exhaustion, but the rewards were paying off. I soon began developing strategies for taking on new cases, including a major employment discrimination case, *Sheppard v. Consolidated Edison of New York*, which challenged the glass ceiling for Blacks at Consolidated Edison. Alan Fuchsberg of the Jacob D. Fuchsberg Law Firm and Daniel Alterman of Alterman & Boop, PC, joined in the effort in litigating the case and helped lend to a successful conclusion. I also became involved in *Rumiche v. New York State Higher Education Services Corporation*, another class action lawsuit, in a joint pact with several legal services offices. The case was effective in obtaining monetary relief for thousands of students who were victims of trade school fraud when their schools closed, leaving them holding unpaid loans for which they never received the education promised.

Soon after, I was dating again. I met a young lady at church. We quickly learned that we had once lived in the same housing apartment complex, worked directly across the street from each other, and shared birthdays seven days apart. It also did not hurt that she was very smart, attractive, elegant, well-dressed, and possessed a great sense of humor. As much as I thought she was godsent, I was cautious. I proceeded slowly and tried to learn every detail about her. Years later, we married. My lovely wife, Charisse, has been at my side since. I was doubly blessed to also gain a stepson in the process, who, too, has enriched my life since he was a little child.

The summer of 1995, the center suffered dramatic cuts to its budget, resulting in layoffs of nearly the entire full-time staff that was on a regular funded line. This sent me to the unemployment line. As I stood in line at the unemployment office to apply for benefits, I wondered aloud what I was doing in an unemployment line with all my skills. In that moment, instead of indulging in self-pity, I became indignant about controlling my life. I had always given thought to having my own law office, and here was my chance. When I arrived at the front of the line, I was told about a special program that would allow me to go into business for myself and get some assistance from the Labor Department.

Shortly after, I signed a lease for office space to begin my law practice in Manhattan, at 15 Park Row, directly across the street from city hall, although I would eventually relocate to the South Street Seaport. I felt proud. Days later, I returned to enroll in the special program for businesses. The Labor Office accepted my application and allowed me to participate in the business training program. But when I finished, I was told I could not receive any financial assistance because I had already signed a lease to start my business when the application for the program was filed. So much for being ambitious. Still, I saw a light at the end of the tunnel, as I have always been able to find a light even in the direst situations. I determined that despite this setback, I would still commence my private law practice. Since I would not be considered a participant in the program, I considered it a blessing to have received the valuable free training from the State yet not be required to file the lengthy monthly reports.

Soon after, several of my friends assisted in conducting a wonderful office warming party and immediately started sending clients.

I also obtained a wonderful secretary, whom I shared. She taught me how to use important business applications on the computer. After several months of operation, I felt relaxed and comfortable being on my own when I learned that the person I was renting from had not been paying the rent, though he had been accepting my money, which I paid timely. The sheriff arrived with an eviction notice and told me I had to move immediately.

At first, I thought it was a big mistake. I wondered how someone I liked and trusted would withhold such critical information from me and place my entire business at risk. I told the sheriff that I was an innocent party and begged his indulgence in permitting me several days to find a place to relocate. To my surprise and satisfaction, he agreed. I immediately went to the court to research the case and learned that the guy had been many months behind in his rent and was at risk of eviction when my lease was signed. Had I known this information at the time, I would have never rented from him. Since the court papers did not appear to present a single defense in his behalf, I was relegated to accepting the fact that this eviction was going forward.

As I was walking back to the office from the courthouse, I thought this was quite an obstacle but surely not one that I could not overcome. I prayed for a solution. When I returned to the office building, the answer was in front of me. When I was an attorney with Legal Aid, I had always made a point of speaking to everyone, including the building custodians. As a result, they grew to know me quite well. Joe, a custodian, whom I met at the beginning of my career with the Legal Aid Society, was now the custodian at 15 Park Row. I had not seen him in the building before. However, he stood at the building entrance, as if waiting to assist me. I immediately approached and told him of my new law practice and my embarrassing circumstances. He offered to inquire with other tenants in the building on my behalf.

When I arrived at the office the following Monday to begin moving my property, he informed me that he had two prospective offices. I interviewed at both and chose Koob & Magoolaghan, a civil rights litigation firm on the penthouse floor of the building.

Elizabeth Koob and Joan Magoolaghan provided me a modest rent, a good space, and a receptionist. I could not ask for better, but it did get better. My business boomed. It was very successful. I received a wide variety of cases, had good clients, and was getting paid wonderfully for my work. It felt good to be my own boss as well as responsible for my own destiny. My relationship with the staff and partners of Koob & Magoolaghan also blossomed into a wonderful professional and personal friendship. In the course of our many discussions, I also learned that the partners of the firm, Elizabeth Koob and Joan Magoolaghan, were previously attorneys with Legal Services of New York, although our paths had never before intersected.

I would be remiss not to mention Zenida Gonzalez, the office manager. She was outstanding. Though tasked only with answering my phone, she voluntarily took on countless other tasks for me, including consoling nervous clients, helping keep me abreast of appointments, and assisting me in locating sometimes hard-to-find forms. She made running my office much easier and certainly much more enjoyable.

However, as many attorneys in private practice know, although private practice can be very enjoyable, one of the biggest disadvantages is what I refer to as "the roller-coaster effect." When business is good, it is truly good; the money is coming in and the business is operating smoothly. But when business is slow, you never know what's going to happen. You even have to wonder if you are going to break even for the month. Private practice can present a constant roller-coaster effect, no matter how long you have been in the business. In the early years, I quite naively thought the roller-coaster effect would end with increased experience on my part. Unfortunately, it did not, thus requiring me to exercise considerable patience through the ebbs and flows.

As a private practitioner, I had many glorious moments representing clients. I represented clients in a wide variety of civil cases, including landlord/tenant, consumer, personal injury, contracts, employment discrimination, and family law. I also handled several criminal cases. The work brought me pleasure, especially the cases that presented a real challenge. And there was nothing like seeing the smile on the face of a happy client.

In one of my earliest cases in private practice, I represented a teacher who was wrongfully terminated because of her age. We prevailed both in state and federal court. She was elated, as was I. And there was nothing like the joy experienced when, at her request, I escorted her back to school on her first day of reinstatement. She was truly deserving. I felt tremendous joy having helped contribute to her return to work and saving her career and reputation in the process.

After this success, word spread like wildfire about my commitment and success on behalf of teachers. As a result, I represented many teachers in age and racial discrimination cases and usually obtained successful results. However, on occasion, I also met teachers who were beyond my help because their transgressions were too great to overcome. In those cases, I honestly advised them of their options and respectfully declined to take their cases. There were also teachers who were wronged but did not have enough evidence to support their cases. I tried to assist them by providing advice about other money-saving options. I have found that clients usually appreciate the truth, even if it is not something they initially want to hear. Therefore, I made it my practice to tell all my clients the truth rather than try to bolster the likely outcome of their cases, only for them to be surprised later.

I also represented parties of all income levels in divorce cases. My personal observation and experiences reflect that parties involved in divorce tend to be very emotionally involved, regardless of their financial status. This made divorce cases very tricky and somewhat complicated to handle because lawyers are expected to maintain professionalism and not become attached to the clients. Meanwhile, the clients want to know that their lawyers understand what they are personally experiencing, thus creating a tension for the lawyer between being an observant professional or an active intervener.

So too, as much as divorcing parties, regardless of which side you represent, claim the other spouse is at fault and how much a divorce would improve their lives, I have rarely seen a divorced client celebrate the divorce. I suspect this is because most people realize that even if they no longer want to be together, the divorce evidences there has been a failure on some level on the part of both parties, whether it be failure to effectively communicate, mend differences, or otherwise. Of course, there are also the exceptions to the rule where the parties should never have been together at all, such as is the case of abuse or domestic violence. However, one never knows what attracts people or keeps them together in the face of all wisdom to the contrary.

Although most of my clients had been truly interesting and very exciting to work with, others had been difficult. Two situations stand out in this area. Most difficult are clients who foresee themselves getting a truckload of money for a case that merits a great deal less. Trying to convince clients of what they are entitled to under the law can be an arduous task because often people think their suffering is worth a lot more than what might be considered reasonable under the law. The other situation is the client who wants a big payday but refuses to do anything to assist the attorney in moving the case along and constantly complains about such simple matters as the need to show up in court for scheduled appearances.

Then there is the client that wants work done but does not want to pay for it. I have experienced and heard so many of these stories from attorneys you would think it is a contagious disease. Clients want assistance and often forget attorneys have more than one case and need other income to survive. However, when the bill is presented, the question arises as to why it costs so much. Well, life is not free, nor is everything free good.

There is also the client who simply has no clue about anything. I once represented such a client in an employment discrimination case. I explained the likelihood of winning or losing the case from the outset and the amount she could expect to receive. The case continued to trial. The jury came back with a very significant award, much more than I anticipated. Instead of thanking me, she cursed me in front of the jury. The judge then vacated the entire jury award. And in the process, she and I lost a lot of money because I surely was not going to represent her on appeal, nor did she use the foresight of following through on her appeal as I had recommended.

Normally I would have appealed, and had I done so, we probably would have won. Instead, the client took actions which were averse to me continuing to represent her, and I withdrew from the case. Shortly after, a landmark case was issued by the US Supreme Court, which supported her position. Instead, I was left scratching my head in disbelief and contemplating what could have been. Years later she called me to apologize, but there was no means to recover from the damage she had inflicted.

CHAPTER 8

Confronting a Health Challenge with Grace and Uncompromising Faith

In early 2005, after ten years in private practice, I faced a challenge that required me to fight mentally and physically for survival. On March 14, 2005, I was diagnosed with cancer. It was drastic news, and I was hardly prepared for it. I had recently married Charisse and not a full year had passed since our blissful wedding ceremony. I wondered how this could be. After all, I was still young, with many years left to live. Young people my age usually did not get prostate cancer, except in rare cases. But on this dreadful day, I learned that my biopsy had come back positive for prostate cancer.

I had suspected that there was a problem when my test results were not readily available and the doctor's office told me "it had to be graded." I could not help but to wonder what was being graded. And then it hit me—they were trying to grade my cancer before telling me the diagnosis. Still, I held out hope until I received the dreadful news. I was at work at the time, and although curious, I was extremely afraid to call and inquire. I attempted to call several times and instead hung the phone up. Then I wondered if I could live with the possibility of knowing I had cancer without doing anything about it. I also wondered how I might handle such drastic news. I quickly came to my senses and made the phone call. When I received the news, it hit me like a sledgehammer, hard and uncompromising. Though I was devastated, I did my best to remain composed.

I prayed for strength in handling the situation. Then, I wondered who I should break the news to first. It would be heart-wrenching for anyone I called. I wanted very much to call my wife first. I thought I owed her the courtesy since she would be on the frontline and most affected by having to deal with this issue daily until I was cured. But I decided I could not break such bad news to her at work. I just did not think it would be fair to put her in that position at work. She might not be able to handle it.

Instead, I called my mother. I knew this would be hard for her too, but who best to understand my current pain than my mother, who herself experienced and survived cancer? My mother had been diagnosed with pancreatic cancer five years earlier. She successfully survived surgery, chemotherapy, and radiation, and was on the rebound and spiritually sound. I thought my mother was very strong and could provide me comfort in handling such shocking news. I badly needed to hear words of inspiration, not words of sorrow about my circumstances. I did not want people to feel sorry for me. I desperately needed a cure and wanted to connect with people who could assist me in getting cured, physically and psychologically.

Hesitantly, I dialed my mother's telephone number, feeling a bit guilty about having to bring her bad news, particularly bad news which she would have no control over. She picked up the telephone and, as only a mother could, sensed immediately that something was wrong. She asked if everything was all right. As my normal response, I said yes. Figuratively, I was all right, but mentally I was a wreck. I just did not want to burden her with anything to be worrying about. She had enough pain to deal with on her own. She had back surgery, followed by knee replacement surgery, and then cancer, which ironically, she was to visit the doctor the same week to ascertain her five-year cure status. She asked again what was wrong, and I responded, "I have cancer." This was the worst news I have ever had to share with my mother. Because she previously had to endure a cancer procedure where her entire digestive system was removed, cleared of cancer, and reassembled, I knew this was probably the worst news she could hear about her child other than death.

After I uttered the words, I waited for the response. She must have been as devastated as I. However, to my delight, she handled it well. Instead of crying out in outrage, she quickly responded, "You can beat cancer just as you beat other bad circumstances in your life." It was a delight to hear this and just what I needed to hear at that moment. Her composure under such difficult circumstances immediately brought me inspiration and great determination. As we ended the conversation, I was comforted with the fact that God would see me through, just as he had seen my mother through her illness. This was my prayer and my desire.

When I went home, I broke the news to my wife. I was glad that I had waited until she arrived home because she thought I was joking. We had joked about many things before, but never had I ever joked about being ill. Still, the fact that she took it as a joke made breaking the news easier. She smoked for many years. So I constantly encouraged her to quit smoking to avoid acquiring cancer. She also enjoyed some of the less healthy foods. In contrast, I usually exercised, did not smoke, drink alcohol, or eat many fatty foods, except for sweets and ice cream. I also visited doctors regularly. Consequently, she considered me to be the healthier of the two of us. Thus, it was inconceivable to her that I would be diagnosed with cancer.

When I told her of my diagnosis, she asked me several times if I was serious before she realized that this was not a joke, although I truly wished it were. It just did not seem real that I would have cancer, and I wondered if somehow a mistake had been made in my diagnosis. But when I visited my urologist two weeks later, he dashed any hopes of a mistake.

My appearance at the doctor's office seemed to be surrounded by secretive discussions among the staff. It felt strange. In the past, the staff had been friendly and happy in my presence, but not this day. This day they were unusually serious and somber. They took an x-ray of my pelvic area then escorted me to the doctor's personal office. They had never invited me to the doctor's personal office before, and I did not want to be in his personal space that day, instead of an examination room, because surely it meant I was going to get some very bad news. It is now obvious that the same news could have been given to me in an examination room. However, that day, I just knew that going into his office meant something very serious was about to occur. I felt it strongly in my conscious.

Minutes later, the doctor came in, advised me of the diagnosis, the grade of cancer, and immediately recommended a manual radical prostatectomy. He then handed me an article he wrote, describing the surgery in gruesome detail. Just seeing the manner of cuts was a turnoff. He also advised me that my report had already been reviewed by Johns Hopkins Medical Center and confirmed, thus dashing any hope that an error had been made. Hearing the news in this fashion hit me like a ton of bricks. I was not able to maintain my composure. I was unable to handle the bad news, especially while being told I had few options. Surely, this news could have been presented a little less mechanically.

Between March 14 and my arrival at the doctor's office, I had begun researching the different methods of treating prostate cancer as well as the side effects.

This was the beginning of my process in reading every book possible, internet articles, and talking with every person I could that had any experience with prostate cancer. Consequently, I knew surgery could have some very serious side effects, not the least of which might include incontinence and impotence. After I composed myself, I presented these questions to the urologist and was told not to worry about it. "It should not be a problem." However, I knew with surgery, no matter how much I wanted to ignore the potential side effects, these were serious matters to consider that might impact my life. Therefore, I told the doctor I would seek other opinions before deciding.

My original intentions were to seek other opinions from doctors, both urologists and radiologists, who, like my doctor, were distinguished in their fields. However, the more I read, the more information I desired and the more answers to questions I needed to pursue. Eventually, I found myself visiting a multitude of radiologists and urologists. The radiologists, almost universally, recommended radiology and/or seed implants. The urologists, almost universally, recommended surgery. I was initially disinclined to do surgery, thinking it posed the greatest risk of side effects. However, during one of my many visits to doctors, I saw a radiologist at Hackensack University Medical Center. After discussing my low-grade cancer and my age, the doctor indicated he would never perform radiation on me as a first option because of my young age and the low-grade cancer. He stated, honestly, that it would not be in my interest because radiation has too many side effects. I was shocked at his opinion, since he failed to offer me any assistance. Yet I was delighted with his honesty.

I later visited a popular Manhattan hospital where I saw a radiologist and urologist. The radiologist, who had also treated a former mayor of the city of New York, was extremely enthusiastic about doing seeds on me, maybe even a little too enthusiastic, such that I wondered whether he was really telling the truth. Since I needed a urologist and a radiologist to implant seeds, I requested and was referred to a urologist at the same hospital. The urologist was low key. He explained my options and told me to come back when ready, whether the choice was seeds or surgery. He also suggested that I may want to return for another biopsy to see what my status was.

In June, after my birthday, I returned to the hospital for another biopsy. Days after the biopsy, I grew very sick. This experience was unlike any biopsy I had previously experienced. I became feverish, vomiting, weak, and had extensive urinary frequency.

I found myself visiting the bathroom nearly every fifteen minutes amid excruciating pain. I did not mind visiting doctors when necessary, although I had never previously been admitted to a hospital. Somehow, I knew my first time was near. I could not wait to get to a hospital.

I called a physician and arranged to be admitted to a hospital immediately. I was diagnosed with urosepsis and remained in the hospital for several days. Ironically, I always knew it was possible cancer could cause my early demise. However, I could not, and did not, anticipate that a simple biopsy would place me perilously close to death long before I would receive any treatment for cancer, as was the case.

I learned of the diagnosis by a note left on my table by a doctor or nursing staff overnight. I guess the hospital had assumed a doctor would get an opportunity to discuss the diagnosis with me before I read the note. Being an early riser, I awoke at 5:00 a.m. to find the note on my table. I read it carefully and saw the diagnosis. However, sometimes the less you know the better. I casually continued to read through the information sheet, and when I read the passage about sepsis causing death unless the proper antibiotic cure is administered in time, I became very alarmed. It was the first time I realized I might die from something other than cancer, and the threat was imminent and very real.

When the doctor arrived to share the bad news with me around 8:00 a.m., unknown to him, I had already read the diagnosis sheet, in detail. He reviewed the diagnosis with me and told me the hospital was unable to identify an effective antibiotic but would continue to work on it. Then he let the hammer fall, telling me if an effective antibiotic was not identified within twenty-four hours, I would not survive the experience. I wanted to scream out in agony, but I was speechless. Seeing no response from me, he asked if I understood what he said. I answered yes. He left without uttering another word. Then it hit me—he just told me I might die. And I wondered if he always acted so casually in giving his patients bad news. I could not help thinking either he was as certain as I about a positive outcome or he was grossly indifferent to what I was going through. My next thought was *I am not going to accept that. God brought me too far to leave me now.* I immediately prayed for a cure and for a quick recovery. I worried no more.

When I awoke the next day and was feeling better, I knew my prayer had been answered. No doctor confirmed such, but I felt it in my spirit, and I graciously thanked God for granting me another day. The hospital chaplain and I crossed paths in the hallway less than one hour later. He looked at me and smiled. I told him how good it was to see him. At that moment, I thought it was great to see anyone at all. However, I was delighted that the first person I saw was a chaplain. He asked if there was anything he could do for me, as if he knew God had just delivered me from peril. I told him I just wanted to learn more about God and asked him to bring me a good book. He promptly returned with a wonderful religious instruction book, exactly what I needed. Unlike the Bibles, which I had frequently read, the book provided extensive details about the books and chapters of the bible. It was perfect for the occasion.

Surprisingly and quite strangely, the hospital never told me a cure was found. But days later, I returned home, after the hospital threaded an intravenous line in my arm near my heart for twice daily self-administration of antibiotics for four weeks. Despite the nuisance of having an intravenous line placed in my arm, I was truly grateful for being able to walk out of the hospital alive.

That September, I opted to have a robotic prostatectomy at Hackensack University Medical Center. This surgery is a robot-assisted removal of the prostate. At the time, this was considered a new procedure used only at a few hospitals nationwide. However, it quickly gained popularity for its effectiveness. Selecting robotic surgery was a difficult choice for me because I was not one to experiment with my body. However, the results of robotic surgery were very appealing and simply could not be ignored. Unlike conventional prostate surgery, which involved a large cut across the abdomen, significant loss of blood, and a long recovery period, robotic surgery involved small incisions the size of a dime which usually disappear, with little or no loss of blood, quick recovery, and a better surgical field. Thus, if surgery was necessary, robotic surgery appeared to be the better choice for me.

Still, although radiation and seeds appeared to be less preferable for a person of my young age, I wondered about the outcome of such if I chose one of those procedures. Would I be fine initially and worry about the side effects sneaking up on me later? And if the radiation seeds or radiation did not work, would my options then be severely limited? The answer appeared to be yes. And so, if nothing else, at least if the robotic operation failed, I would get another chance by doing radiation treatments. I therefore decided to proceed with the surgery.

On the day of surgery, I prayed for blessings for myself, my family and friends, and all the medical personnel involved with my care. I prayed that every hand that touched my body be blessed. After, the nurse took my blood pressure. Although I was nervous, my blood pressure was excellent, so much so that the nurses joked about my blood pressure being better than theirs. When I entered the operating room, I immediately went to sleep. When I awoke, I felt great. It was an astonishing feeling to wake up and realize that I had been given another chance at life, and I thanked God for the opportunity.

When I arrived at my room, the doctors came to visit. I saw excitement in their eyes. They told me the surgery went well and that surprisingly my blood pressure never changed throughout the entire four-hour surgery. Maybe they did not understand it and had never seen anything like it before, but I knew this was a blessing from God, as was the fact that the Spirit stepped in to intervene when the doctor thought he might have to convert my surgery to the conventional method due to the difficulty he faced in removing the prostate. As the doctor explained to me, "at that critical moment, I suddenly gained patience, and the rest went smoothly." It may have surprised him, but it was no surprise to me, that nothing is too hard for my spiritual Father.

The day after surgery I was up walking, though very slowly. To my surprise, I had to learn to walk again. At that moment, I truly appreciated having previously known how to walk, which is something we all eventually take for granted. I was anxious to walk for more than a few baby steps at a time. However, even walking around the nurse station took great effort and felt like a mile. I did not know at the time that during this type of surgery, the patient is also filled with gas to expand the area. As a result, I felt extremely bloated. When I looked in the mirror, I noticed that I looked like I was about to deliver a baby. My abdomen was terrifyingly huge and overstretched. At that moment, I wondered how women tolerate their abdomens being bloated for many months during pregnancy when I could barely tolerate it for a day. Days later, I was overjoyed to see my abdomen resume to its normal size.

I left Hackensack Medical Center with a catheter in place. I had been warned about the catheter by other people who had them. I was elated that the catheter was placed while I was asleep prior to surgery, because the placement of a catheter is not a pleasant experience, as I have learned and experienced several times since.

I had been prepared to have it in place two weeks and could not imagine bearing the pain and inconvenience for that long. Therefore, I was also delighted when the doctor told me that the catheter would only be in place one week. Still, for the next week, the pain of that catheter was excruciating. I could not help but wonder if this experience was intended to further elevate my comprehension of the dynamics of pain. If so, the lesson was well received. I felt helpless and prayed for strength to get me through it.

I felt even more helpless one week later when the catheter was taken out.

Though extremely relieved to get rid of the catheter, that day, I was totally incontinent.

I prayed for strength, indulgence, and an immediate remedy. Fortunately, I was alone that day.

I found I just could not handle the experience, mentally or physically. Doctors had tried to prepare me for this possibility, but there was nothing like experiencing it. Suddenly it struck me—if this continued, I would have to give up my way of life as I once knew it, and I was totally unprepared to do that. I tried to do everything to get my mind off my condition by convincing myself it was just temporary. God forbid this condition lasted for any length of time. I was utterly unprepared to deal with it.

Miraculously, the next morning, I was totally continent. This is rare, but I was extremely grateful for the blessing. I was also grateful at that point for not experiencing some of the numerous other side effects of prostate cancer. Unfortunately, my early gratification was short-lived. Weeks later, I learned that radiation was required because my Prostate Specific Antigen (PSA) did not reach the targeted level after surgery. This was a surprise since I had opted for surgery to avoid radiation. Here I was having to take the same chances and incumbent risks all over again. I wondered if I was prone to bad luck or whether there was a character-building lesson in this experience for me. Instead of choosing the path of despair, I adopted a positive attitude concerning my survival no matter what obstacles lay ahead.

The following months I searched for a radiation oncologist that could provide me the most recent technology available, intensity modulated radiation therapy, which was reported to give precise radiation doses to the affected area while limiting exposure to other parts of the body. Initially, I met with specialists at a well-known hospital in New York, where the doctor appeared totally insensitive in describing the methods used and in answering my questions about the side effects. He showed no concern whatsoever for my desire to remain continent and for limited radiation exposure on my rectum to avoid the high incidence of rectal cancer for such patients. This turned out to be a matter of good fortune because I never returned and instead went to meet with medical personnel at the Rahway Regional Cancer Center in New Jersey.

The staff at RRCC were so generous and kind on the telephone it was breathtaking. The same level of professionalism and sensitivity was exhibited during my consultation with the doctor. He explained every detail of my medical status, as well as the radiation process, and warmly welcomed my questions. Soon after, I learned that the entire staff exhibited the same high level of skill, sensitivity, patience, and can-do spirit. It was agonizing to leave my law practice every day for several months in the middle of the day to attend radiation sessions. However, the RRCC staff helped turn a bad situation into a very tolerable experience. Though sullied by my circumstances, I was always excited about visiting and talking with the wonderful staff at RRCC.

Dr. Eric Karp and staff willingly went above and beyond. During one occasion, when the radiation machine broke down for more than two days, the doctor treated his patients to gift certificates for lunch or dinner. Although not requested or expected, it was a remarkable gesture, as was his urging that I call him any time of the day or night if necessary. I remain forever grateful for the services of the RRCC.

As I was undergoing radiation treatment, it became readily evident to me that cancer centers should consider changing their names. There is no denying that the word *cancer* carries a stigma. However, the purpose of these centers is to destroy bad cells and restore them with good cells, hence *cell regeneration center* might be more appropriate. Imagine signs at these places reading cell regeneration center instead of cancer. This would encourage patients in their outcomes and better describe the work that takes place inside. Quite frankly, I did not like cancer signs even before I learned that I had cancer. The signs always beckoned a sad feeling within me about the circumstances of people who required these services. Now, I was one of such patients. Consequently, changing the name might help lend to a more positive image of the work taking place inside while further encouraging patients.

Also, no matter what anyone tells you, radiation can be an unpleasant experience. Often, treatments are required daily and occasionally for months at a time. The experience itself requires lying under exposure of an x-ray machine and can best be described as human microwaving. The person lies or sits on the table while a machine targets the respective areas with beams. And yes, you will likely feel the effect no matter what anyone tells you, whether it is internal burning, exhaustion, dizziness, chafed skin, diarrhea, or urinary frequency.

However, honestly, I probably had as good an experience as can be expected from radiation. I did not experience any of the normal side effects until the final weeks of treatment when I found myself making frequent trips to the restroom, especially at night. This was extremely annoying. Fortunately, I never required many hours of sleep. Many days and nights I also worked or tried to sleep through the pain I was experiencing. My radiation experiences taught me what a "pain in the butt" really feels like. Consequently, I learned to no longer take for granted the absence of pain and to better appreciate the significance of my bodily systems operating with precision.

The pain and frequency continued long after the radiation treatments terminated.

As was explained to me, radiation requires more time to wear off than healing after surgery. Fortunately, the effects lessened, although less quickly, as the days wore on. In the interim, there was lots of strain and pain as the cells in my body sought to regenerate and heal following their onslaught with radiation. Fortunately, my PSA bottomed at zero, evidencing remission.

However, just as I was beginning to take comfort in my cure in November 2006, I learned of a new problem as a result of the surgery and/or radiation. As the months passed, the problem grew worse. By February 2007, I landed back in the hospital with kidney failure, as a result of my bladder not emptying completely. Over the next several weeks and months, I became a regular at two hospitals for bladder and kidney failure due to accumulated scar tissue from my medical procedures.

My doctors were astounded that I could keep going while engaged in full kidney failure and recover completely. I was not as surprised since I knew that all things are possible through the exercise of faith and prayer. After hearing the doctors and nurses talk about what usually happens to people in my circumstances, I was truly elated that God bestowed his blessings and granted me complete recovery each time. Still, the experience wore heavily on me. It was frightening. Every time I thought I was clear to reengage in my regular activities, I found myself facing a new setback.

I felt the greatest impact on my birthday, June 14, 2007, when I learned that yet another surgery would be necessary. I was not prepared to be told that another surgery was required despite having had surgery, radiation, and a near-death experience with sepsis. But I refused to give up, although one cancer expert told me I would have to live with a catheter for the rest of my life because it was going to take a miracle to correct the situation. When the doctor told me this, I told him if a miracle was necessary, God was going to grant me a miracle. I truly believed this. There was no point in trying to convince a doctor who had no medical or spiritual hope to assist me in finding a solution to my recovery. So, I departed his office and proceeded to locate a doctor who believed I could be healed.

I was anxious about taking the next step. I intensified my prayers and sought another blessing. This experience led me back to Premier Urology Associates, a tight-knit group of very fine urology surgeons. The doctors at Premier Urology were strongly of the opinion that my bladder retention with secondary kidney failure could be corrected. This gave me comfort, and I opted to have the surgery.

In my previous encounters with Dr. Mark Miller, he always explained the procedures and alternatives in detail, and chose the least restrictive options. It also did not hurt that he possessed a kilowatt personality. After speaking with him about my concerns, he assured me he could likely resolve the issue. He also informed me of the risks and that he would approach the matter in steps. I fully trusted that he would approach the surgery conservatively. Otherwise, I would be relegated to a catheter for life, or worse. Although I never imagined that it would take three or four surgeries to get the job done, he did an excellent job and achieved the desired outcome. I remain truly grateful for his services.

After my bladder and kidney issues resolved, the PSA continued bottoming out at zero. It had been a long journey, but God surely made it worth the wait. I was relieved, as were the many others who prayed for me. The tremendous weight on my shoulders was lifted, and I was again ready to return to my previous activities.

CHAPTER 9

New Storms Arrive before a Lifetime Blessing

As I was about to take a sigh of relief from my medical issues, I learned another law firm would be taking over the lease of my law office suite at the South Street Seaport in New York City, from Koob & Magoolaghan. I had rented space with Koob & Magoolaghan since my days on Park Row and nearly the entire time I was in private practice. We had developed a warm relationship not only as colleagues but very good friends. I truly enjoyed their presence. However, the firm had decided to relocate to Yonkers. I was saddened to see them leave. We had some good times together, celebrating professional and personal achievements as well as spending leisure time. My first and only cruise on a sailboat was down the Hudson River with the Koob & Magoolaghan Firm, and they were an amazingly exciting group of people to hang out with, in the office or otherwise.

I had also observed them develop the South Street Seaport office from scratch, restoring it from an old meat warehouse into a very modernized office space, which they themselves created with the assistance of an architect. I can still remember the day they told me we would relocate from Park Row to a meat warehouse at the South Street Seaport. My immediate thoughts were what a very ambitious group of people. When I saw the plans, I was extremely impressed with their creativity in designing the space. When we moved in, I was elated beyond belief at how beautiful the offices were, several of which included skylights. And my rent remained modest, for a prime tourist location. I could not ask for more.

The new firm that later acquired the lease space was, however, more profit orientated and much less personable. The head of the firm also made very clear to me that I could not presume it would work out a rental arrangement with me unless I was willing to pay a substantial rental increase. As we engaged in the process of negotiating a rental agreement, the firm began renting spaces in the office to whomever it could, even to the point of renting desk space in the corridors.

A week before Christmas, we reached a written compromise agreement that included a substantial rent increase. I was delighted that we were able to reach an agreement, although it placed increased financial pressure on me. However, the new contract arrangement was short-lived. Even after signing a new lease with me, the firm continued soliciting others to rent my office space for a substantially higher amount and making my stay very uncomfortable. Eventually, I grew tired of the situation and decided to relocate. My leap of faith immediately paid off. I found a rental space nearby with a wonderful attorney at a reasonable rent.

Jorge Sorote, like myself, had many years of experience practicing law. He was a very affable people person. Mr. Sorote and his paralegal and I developed an immediate friendship. As a result of our relationship, we were able to discuss a wide range of professional and personal topics with ease. And in the process, I learned a great deal and grew wiser.

As I was still settling into the new office, in July 2008, my mother suddenly grew ill. Having previously successfully survived two knee replacements, back surgery, and pancreatic cancer, which she handled gracefully, my brothers, sisters, and I were optimistic there would be a positive outcome. After all, she had previously beat the odds in quickly recovering from her previous medical challenges. We soon learned this time would be different.

My mother's pancreatic cancer had resurfaced, after nearly eight years in remission, invading her lungs. Shortly after, she departed this life on August 3, 2008, in Clearwater, Florida, where she had relocated two years prior. In many ways, I think she was ready because she did not want to suffer. Still, the result was too difficult to imagine. I thank God for giving me such a wonderful mother and for the many great things she taught me and my siblings about life, prayer and survival. She lived with great dignity and left us in the same fashion. I will always miss her.

After my mother's homegoing services, I returned from Florida days later to a tranquil office. And although I was struggling in my practice to survive in a recession economy, I was meeting my expenses timely. It also helped a great deal that I had a warm and friendly office environment in which to work. The months after passed slowly, as if time stood still in salute to my mother. And frankly, I wondered how I would go on without her counsel, wisdom, and support. Yet I had no choice. I prayed and waited, prayed some more, and waited.

Months later, I was offered a part-time job as a project director with the New York City Bar Association, supervising attorneys who worked as volunteers in the Lawyer-For-A-Day Project in the housing court in New York City. This job gave me the opportunity to meet many fine lawyers, from large and small law firms, who worked as volunteers in the program, interface with court employees of various titles, and supplement my private practice income. I supervised the attorney volunteers in providing brief representation to tenants with pending rent eviction cases. It was extremely rewarding training the attorneys in handling housing court cases, assisting them with resolving the cases and witnessing the gratification of the tenants when their cases were resolved. I enjoyed the job tremendously. This job, along with my private practice, kept me very busy and gave me a renewed spirit.

I also located and reconnected with my daughter, after many years of searching for her. My persistence in making use of the internet technology paid off, and I got to visit my daughter for the first time in many years. As far as I was concerned, things were going very well for me.

But God still had more in store. In June 2009, an elected judicial vacancy became available, and I decided to enter the race.

Admittedly, I was very nervous about running for election, as I had never participated in electoral politics before, and the vacancy was for a countywide seat, which would not be easily achieved. Nevertheless, I was convinced that what God has for me is for me. And I was not going to sit idly by and let someone else claim my blessing. I prayed mightily that all the right people be sent forth to help me in my journey and that I might impress people in a manner that demonstrates my passion and commitment to serve.

The first step was selecting a campaign manager. In this quest, the first person recommended to me informed me that she no longer works in that capacity. The second person, Olanike Alabi, initially turned me down. But in doing so, I told her that although she had already indicated she was reluctant to assist me that God had revealed to me that she would serve in the capacity and we would both be blessed. To my satisfaction, she relented. She accepted the task, and we never looked back. She was a wonderful campaign manager and served with utmost integrity and distinction. We have been good friends since. During that campaign, the then Democratic Party chairperson also aided me by moving all my potential Democratic Party challengers out of the way and helping clear my path for a victory.

In November 2009, I was elected as a judge of the New York City Civil Court and assigned to the courthouse at 141 Livingston Street, in Brooklyn, where I began handling civil cases, effective January 2010. In January 2015, I was appointed Acting Justice of the Supreme Court of the State of New York and began hearing Civil Court and Supreme Court cases during the week and conducting arraignments in criminal court on designated weekends.

Amid this experience, in January 2016, to my surprise, I was appointed the first Black male supervising judge in the history of the New York City Civil Court, Kings County. When I became aware that the position was available, I did not pray for the position. Instead, I prayed that if God could effectively use me in the position that I would be selected. That is exactly what happened.

During my tenure as supervising judge overseeing the operations of the New York City Civil Court in Brooklyn, I comprised a committee to assist me in tackling issues. This committee was representative of mostly every employee group in the building, whether maintenance, security, clerks, stenographers, or judges. We worked hard and closely together to tackle the issues affecting the facilities and the work environment. We were successful in getting the name of the court placed on the building for the first time, resurrecting the flags outside, restoring bathrooms, upgrading the physical facilities, and a large host of other achievements. The judicial and nonjudicial staff also worked tremendously hard to efficiently process a very large volume of cases despite personnel shortages. It was a wonderfully challenging job and a very exciting year. The blessings were truly flowing for me.

Another blessing arrived in November 2016, when I was elected as a justice of the New York State Supreme Court, the state's highest trial court after several years of maneuvering. This was no small achievement since Supreme Court justices could run on multiple party lines, but in New York City the dominant Democratic Party required the support of the county leader and a large majority of the forty-two district leaders. It also was not an inexpensive endeavor since successful candidates typically are required to attend lots of dinners and other events, at their own expense, over a period of years. Consequently, after the November election, I knew I would be departing my position as supervising judge to face new challenges in the Supreme Court, effective January 2017. Although having mixed feelings about leaving so many people at New York City Civil Court that I had developed a deep admiration for, the Supreme Court presented an opportunity I could not resist.

In Supreme Court, I was initially assigned to a part handling motions in cases of all types in which the City of New York and other local government entities were parties. I was also responsible for a trial part for all other matters. By May 2017, I had found my footing and was truly enjoying the work when another challenge presented itself. I was sitting on the bench hearing oral arguments in a case when I discovered that if the attorneys stood on a certain side of the bench, I had difficulty seeing them. I calmly got off the bench and went to chambers to finish the cases.

During the lunch hour, I visited and was examined by an eye doctor who told me my eye was fine. That evening I obtained a second opinion at a hospital emergency room. This doctor also told me my eye was fine and reprimanded me for seeking her out after an "eye doctor with more sophisticated equipment" told me my eye was fine. Two days later, I woke to a worsened condition and visited another hospital emergency room. Moments after, I became totally blind in the affected eye. The emergency room doctor was completely shocked and tried to maintain her composure since only minutes before I had vision, albeit limited. I was devastated but maintained my composure.

The doctor smartly called in an eye specialist that diagnosed me with a complete retinal detachment. It was made clear to me that due to the extent of the detachment, I might never see out of the eye again. I remained blind in the eye for three days before a surgeon was able to reattach the retina in an intricate surgical procedure performed while I was awake. After months of recovery, I still could see little out of the eye. I was diagnosed with a cataract and told to prepare for another surgery. After the cataract was removed, the recovery process began again, with no sight, little sight, and very blurry sight. Just when I thought progress was being made, my doctors discovered that scar tissue had invaded my retina after the surgeries, compromising my vision in the process. And so it was, on to a third surgery to remove the scar tissue, and began the process of no sight, little sight, and blurry sight again, followed by a fourth procedure to remove a film over my eye. As I learned during this process, it takes a seriously long time for the eye to recover. But I thank God that it did. I thank God for all the people who supported me during this difficult time by offering a prayer or words of encouragement.

I also thank Dr. Vincent Ho and Dr. Matthew Hosler for their exceptional skill and professionalism in restoring my vision.

Thanks to the prayers, support, and guidance of so many people, I continue to serve as a justice of the New York State Supreme Court in Brooklyn, New York, where I hear a wide variety of civil cases. I also continue to live a productive, healthy, and very satisfying life. I hope my experiences will serve as some encouragement to others.

God desires that we trust him during good and bad times. Indeed, the COVID-19 viral pandemic that confronted the country would undoubtedly qualify as one of such bad times. As of May 14, 2020, the US had 1,427,243 confirmed cases of COVID-19 and over 85,000 deaths. Many states remained in lockdown, and no vaccine existed. People were being required to wear face masks and to remain six feet apart in public spaces. Many stores were rationing food. Schools and most job sites were closed, and there remained a shortage of hospital beds. By all measures, it was a dire situation. But the country gradually began reopening, state by state, and the country gained inspiration from the fact that most people affected by the virus recovered, although too many lives were lost. This was a crowning moment to test our faith.

Indeed, the true test of character and stamina is not how we handle matters when all is going well but our response to dire situations. The real question is can we be trusted to rely on him when things are not going well? I admit this is not always easy but certainly achievable with godly faith. My vision problems really tested my faith. The blindness in one eye was traumatic beyond measure. The multiple procedures also required tremendous patience. But nothing compares to the joy I experienced as my vision gradually began returning. My prayers were rewarded, and the more I prayed, the better it got.

Life is full of challenges. The real test is how we handle those challenges, whether we give in with a sense of hopelessness or summon our inner strength and think positive to overcome such difficulties. This quality separates the strong from the weak, people of faith from those lacking faith, and the successful from the unsuccessful.

Along the way, some people doubted that much could come of me as a youngster growing up in the public housing projects on Ashmun Street. But I had a different view of myself. I believed, despite my environment; I alone controlled my destiny. Consequently, I confronted the challenges with conviction and a determination to succeed.

Despite my excellent grades and other notable experiences, when some took a dim view of me attending an Ivy League School, I treated this as a challenge to demonstrate that hope and opportunity remains in America for people like myself and found my way to Brown University. I handled the challenge to obtain admission to law school in similar fashion, by summoning and highlighting my strengths and making the case for being deserving of the opportunity. More challenges followed during law school and after, but no matter the challenge, I returned to the basics, being always prayerful and keeping a positive perspective. My approach to dealing with cancer, loss of vision, and other setbacks were the same. This, in turn, led me to a wonderful marriage, restoration of my health, and professional success.

It is not always easy to maintain a positive perspective, but you must. I have achieved the many successes in my personal and professional life as a result of insisting on maintaining a positive attitude, no matter the circumstances. Today, I continue to strive toward new endeavors, new challenges, and new opportunities while keeping my head high. Put God first and remain strong, determined, focused and display a positive attitude regardless of the circumstances. This is my formula for living life against the odds.

ABOUT THE AUTHOR

Reginald A. Boddie is a justice of the New York State Supreme Court and former supervising judge of the New York City Civil Court in Brooklyn, New York. He is the recipient of a host of professional and community service awards. *Living Life against the Odds* provides vivid details of his path to success and the many challenges he confronted along the way. This is a must-read book about determination and perseverance.

CPSIA information can be obtained
at www.ICGtesting.com
Printed in the USA
LVHW081245080422
715704LV00003B/4